TOSEL®

READING SERIES

BASIC

READING 2

International TOSEL Committee

CONTENTS

About TOSEL®

TOSEL (Test of Skills in the English Language) was developed to meet the demand for a more effective assessment of English as a foreign language for learners from specific cultural settings.

TOSEL evaluates and certifies the proficiency levels of English learners, from the age of 4 through adulthood, along with academic and job performance results.

Background

- Other English tests are ineffective in accurately measuring individual abilities
- Overuse of US-dominated testing systems in diverse cultural and educational contexts in the global English language learning market

Functions & Usage

- Assessment is categorized into 7 levels
- Used as a qualification for academic excellence for school admissions
- Used as a test to assess the English proficiency in the corporate and public sectors

Goals

- Create an effective tool for assessing and evaluating the English skills of English language learners
- Implement efficient and accessible testing systems and methods
- Provide constructive and developmental English education guidance

TOSEL® Strength

LEVELED ASSESSMENTS

An established English test system fit for seven different levels according to learners' cognitive development

ACCURATE DIAGNOSIS

A systematic and scientific diagnosis of learners' English proficiency

EXTENSIVE MATERIALS

Supplementary materials to help learners in an EFL environment to prepare for TOSEL and improve their proficiency

SUFFICIENT DATA

Content for each level developed by using data accumulated from more than 2,000,000 TOSEL test takers delegated at 15,000 schools and academies

CLASSIFIED AREAS OF INTELLIGENCE

Content designed to foster and expand the strengths of each student, categorized by the eight areas of intelligence

CONTINUITY

A complete course of English education ranging from kindergarten, elementary school, middle school, high schoool, and up to adults.

HIGH RELIABILITY

A high reliability level (Cronbach's alpha: .904 for elementary school students / .864 for university students) proven by several studies (Oxford University / Modern Language Journal)

SYSTEMATIC & EFFECTIVE ENGLISH EDUCATION

Accurate diagnosis and extensive materials which provide a step-by-step development in English learning, according to the quality of each learner's ability

TOSEL® Level Chart

Seven Separate Assessments

TOSEL divides the test into seven stages, by considering the test takers' cognitive levels, according to different ages. Unlike other assessments based on only one level, TOSEL includes separate assessments for preschool, elementary school, middle school, high school students, and for adults, which also includes both professionals and college students.

TOSEL's reporting system highlights the strengths and weaknesses of each test taker and suggests areas for further development.

COCOON

Suitable for children aged 4-6 (pre-schoolers)

The first step in the TOSEL system, the test is composed of colorful designs and interesting questions to interest young learners and to put them at ease.

Pre-STARTER

Suitable for children aged 7-8 (1st-2nd grades of elementary school)

Evaluates the ability to comprehend simple vocabulary, conversations, and sentences.

STARTER

Suitable for children aged 9-10 (3rd-4th grades of elementary school)

Evaluates the ability to comprehend short sentences and conversations related to everyday situations or topics.

BASIC

Suitable for children aged 11-12 (5th–6th grades of elementary school)

Evaluates the ability to communicate about personal information, daily activities, future plans, and past experiences in written and spoken language.

JUNIOR

Suitable for middle school students

Evaluates the ability to comprehend short paragraphs, practical texts, and speech covering general topics and to participate in simple daily conversations.

HIGH JUNIOR

Suitable for high school students

Evaluates the ability to use English fluently, accurately, and effectively on a wide range of social and academic subjects, as well as the ability to use sentences with a variety of complex structures.

ADVANCED

Suitable for university students and adults

Evaluates the ability to use practical English required for a job or work environment, as well as the ability to use and understand English at the university level.

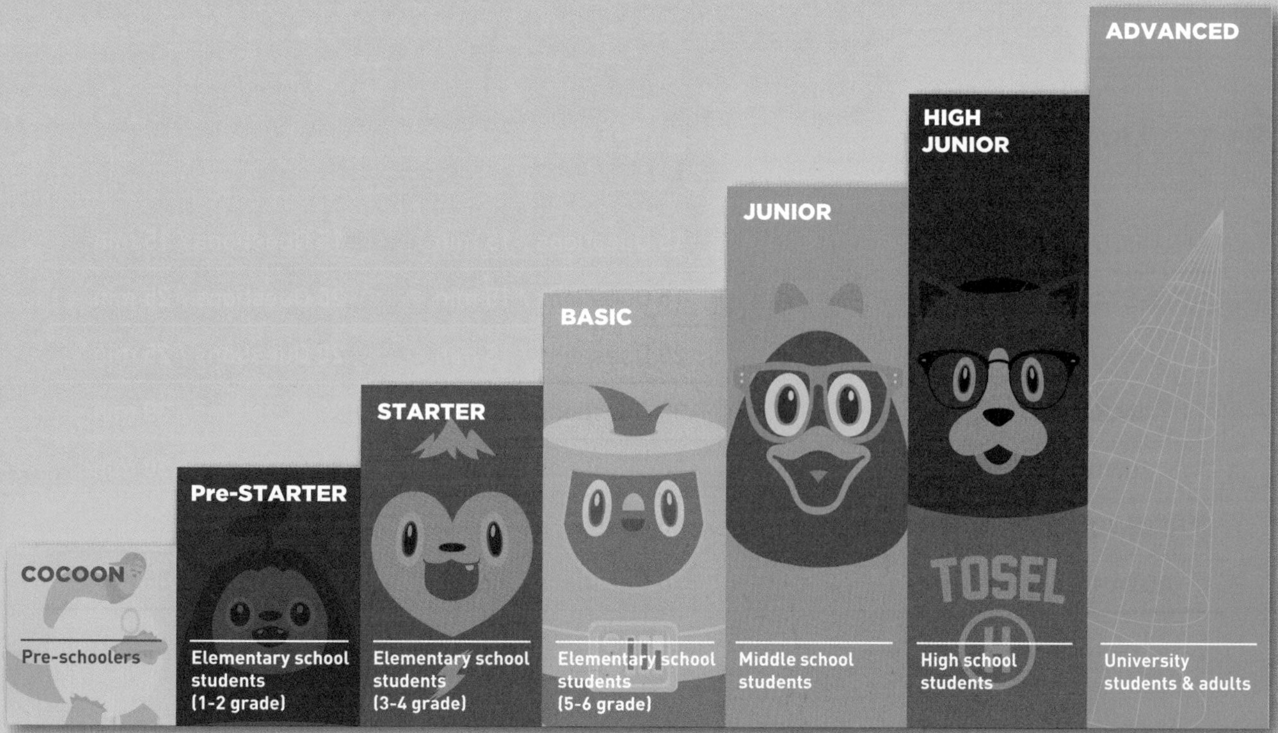

Evaluation

Assessing the Four Skills

TOSEL evaluates the four language skills: reading, listening, speaking and writing, through indirect and direct assessment items.

This system of evaluation is part of a concerted effort to break away from materials geared solely toward grammar and reading-oriented education.

TOSEL Test Information

Level	Score	Grade	Section I Listening & Speaking	Section II Reading & Writing
COCOON	100	1-10	15 Questions / 15 min	15 Questions / 15 min
Pre-STARTER	100		15 Questions / 15 min	20 Questions / 25 min
STARTER	100		20 Questions / 15 min	20 Questions / 25 min
BASIC	100		30 Questions / 20 min	30 Questions / 30 min
JUNIOR	100		30 Questions / 20 min	30 Questions / 30 min
HIGH JUNIOR	100		30 Questions / 25 min	35 Questions / 35 min
ADVANCED	990		70 Questions / 45 min	70 Questions / 55 min

Certificates

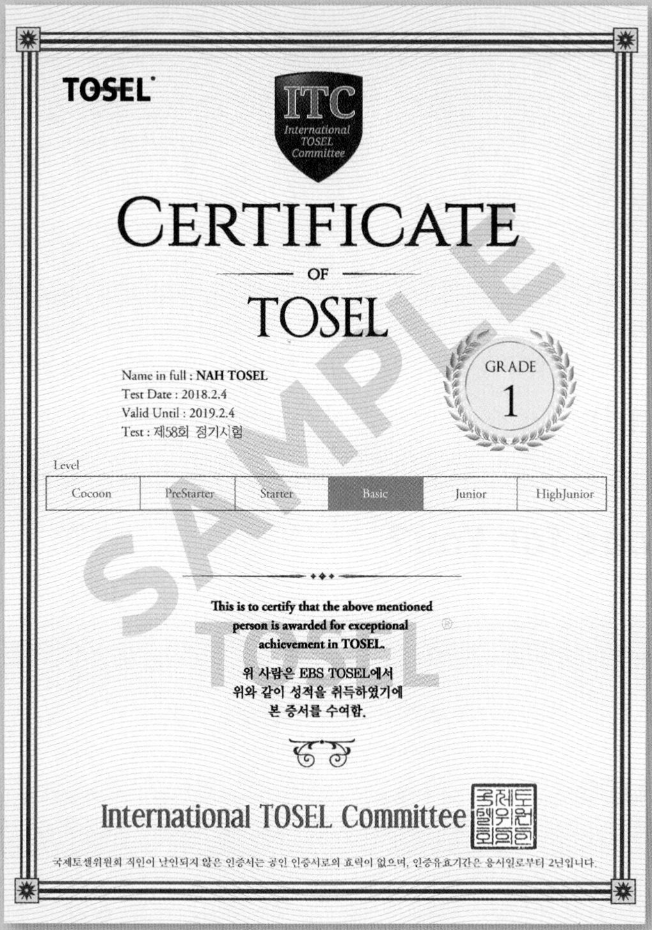

TOSEL Certificate

The International TOSEL Committee officially evaluates and certifies the level of English proficiency of English learners from the age of 4 to adults.

Certified by

Mar. 2010 Korea University
Dec. 2009 The Korean Society of Speech Science
Dec. 2009 The Korea Association of Foreign Language Education
Nov. 2009 The Applied Linguistics Association of Korea
Oct. 2009 The Pan Korea English Teachers Association

CHAPTER 1

Healthy Life

Teacher's Book p.100

UNIT 1

How to Keep Friends

Do you keep friends for a long time?
How long can people be friends?

UNIT 1 How to Keep Friends

We meet new friends all the time. But how can we keep friends for a long time? These three tips can help. First, you can be a good listener. Ask your friend, "How was your day?" Then just listen to the answer! Second, see your friend in person. Online friends are great. But it is also important to see your friends in real life sometimes. You need to do things together. For example, you can go to a park, to a movie, or to a museum. You can play a sport together. Or you can watch videos in your friend's room. Just be together in real life. Third, say "I'm sorry." and "It's okay." Did you have a fight? Say "I'm sorry." Did your friend say "I'm sorry." to you? Maybe you can say, "It's okay." Of course, sometimes friends do not stay friends forever. But these tips can help you keep a friend for a long time.

New Words

tip *n* some advice	good listener *n* ex Are you quiet when your friend is speaking? Maybe you are a good listener.
in person *adv* face-to-face	in real life *adv* not online
have a fight *v* argue	keep *v* have forever

10 minutes

Part A. Sentence Completion

1. Let's go _______ the park. The weather is great!

(A) to
(B) at
(C) on
(D) next

2. Did you _______ a fight?

(A) has
(B) had
(C) have
(D) having

Part B. Situational Writing

3.

Jisu is _______ about the vase.

(A) cold
(B) sorry
(C) tired
(D) happy

4.

Chad and his friends went to a _______ together.

(A) zoo
(B) park
(C) movie
(D) museum

Part C. Practical Reading and Retelling

5. When will Minju NOT meet anyone?

(A) Monday

(B) Tuesday

(C) Wednesday

(D) Friday

6. What is Minju doing on Wednesday?

(A) going to a theater

(B) doing chores in the house

(C) having lunch with her friend

(D) eating a meal with her family

Part D. General Reading and Retelling

We meet new friends all the time. But how can we keep friends for a long time? These three tips can help. First, you can be a good listener. Ask your friend, "How was your day?" Then just listen to the answer! Second, see your friend in person. Online friends are great. But it is also important to see your friends in real life sometimes. You need to do things together. For example, you can go to a park, to a movie, or to a museum. You can play a sport together. Or you can watch videos in your friend's room. Just be together in real life. Third, say "I'm sorry." and "It's okay." Did you have a fight? Say "I'm sorry." Did your friend say "I'm sorry." to you? Maybe you can say, "It's okay." Of course, sometimes friends do not stay friends forever. But these tips can help you keep a friend for a long time.

7. What is the main idea of the passage?
   (A) Friends are not as important as family.
   (B) Friends do not stay friends for a long time.
   (C) One good friend is better than many friends.
   (D) There are ways to keep friends for a long time.

8. Which is NOT a tip in the passage?
   (A) Do things together.
   (B) Listen to your friend.
   (C) Make gifts for your friend.
   (D) Visit your friend in person.

9. What does the passage say about online friends?
   (A) They can be good.
   (B) They are usually bad.
   (C) They have nice photos.
   (D) They sometimes tell lies.

10. According to the passage, when could you say "It's okay."?
   (A) before a big contest
   (B) after a video you like
   (C) when your friend says, "I'm sorry."
   (D) when your dog breaks something

Listening Practice

Listen and write.

MP3 B2-1

How to Keep Friends

We meet new friends all the time. But how can we keep friends for a long time? These three [1] ______ can help. First, you can be a good [2] ______. Ask your friend, "How was your day?" Then just listen to the answer! Second, see your friend [3] ______. Online friends are great. But it is also important to see your friends [4] ______ sometimes. You need to do things together. For example, you can go to a park, to a movie, or to a museum. You can play a sport together. Or you can watch videos in your friend's room. Just be together in real life. Third, say "I'm sorry." and "It's okay." Did you have a [5] ______? Say "I'm sorry." Did your friend say "I'm sorry." to you? Maybe you can say, "It's okay." Of course, sometimes friends do not stay friends forever. But these tips can help you [6] ______ a friend for a long time.

Word Bank

tips	hight	kip
keep	in real life	listener
fight	in person	in puhson
tipps	lisner	in realife

Listen. Pause. Say each sentence.

MP3 B2-1G

Writing Practice

Write the words.

1 ______________ *n* some advice	2 ______________ *n* ex Are you quiet when your friend is speaking? Maybe you are a ______.
3 ______________ *adv* face-to-face	4 ______________ *adv* not online
5 ______________ *v* argue	6 ______________ *v* have forever

Write the words in each blank.

Summary

There are three tips to keep your friends for a ______________ time. First, be a good ______________. Second, see your friend ______________ sometimes. Lastly, say "______________" and "It's okay" after a fight.

Word Puzzle

Complete the word puzzle.

1↓
argue

2→
have forever

3↓
not online

4↓
Are you quiet when your friend is speaking? Maybe you are a ______.

5→
face-to-face

6→
some advice

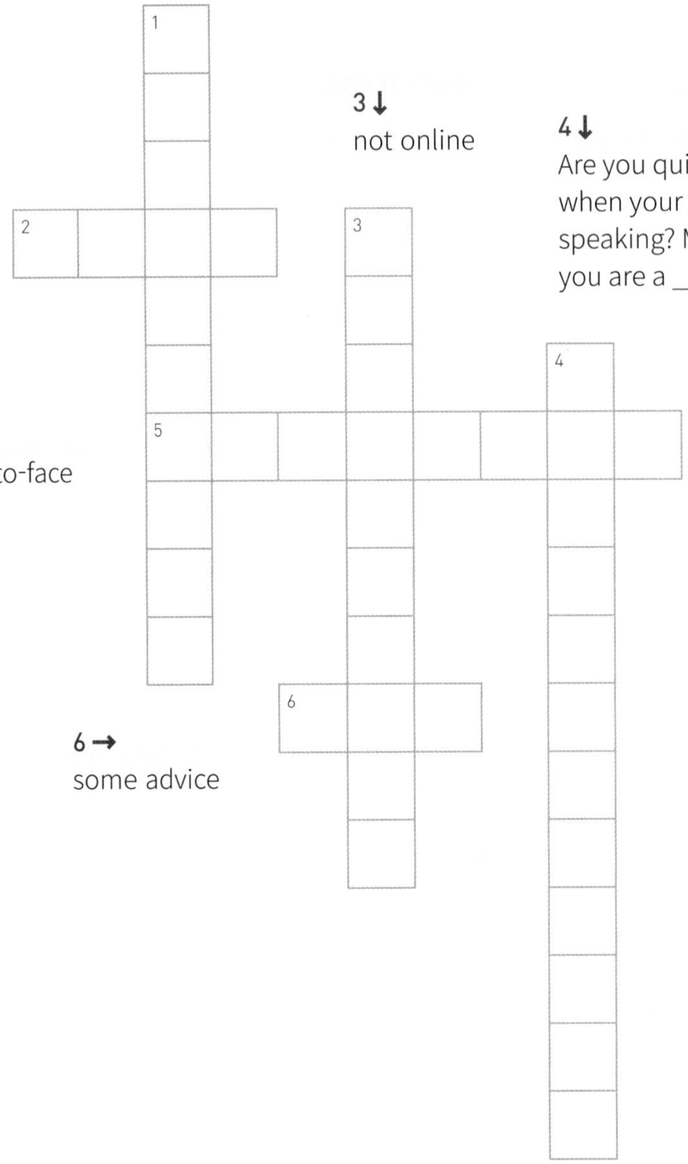

Teacher's Book p.104

UNIT 2

Is Having a Dog Good for You?

Do you have a pet? If not, do you want one?

UNIT 2 Is Having a Dog Good for You?

One Monday morning, Abi's neighbor Mason went to Abi's house. He said, "This is my dog, Thunder. I am going away for one week. Can you take care of Thunder?" Abi looked at Thunder. She did not usually like dogs. But she said, "Sure." After dinner, Abi walked Thunder in the park. He had a lot of energy and tried to smell every tree. He sometimes barked happily at other dogs. Runners in the park noticed Thunder and smiled at him. Children wanted to pet Thunder. That week, Abi walked Thunder every morning and evening. She talked to lots of people in the park. She was never lonely with Thunder. On Saturday, Mason returned from his trip. He went to get Thunder. Abi watched Thunder walk away. She felt sad. She said to Mason, "Thank you for bringing Thunder to me. Life with him was wonderful!"

New Words

notice *v* see	**lonely** *adj* not happy because you are not with other people
have a lot of energy *v* be excited and move around a lot	**bark** *v* make the sound of a dog
pet *v* Is she touching the dog's hair? Then she is petting the dog. 	**wonderful** *adj* really great

Part A. Sentence Completion

1. A _______ water in the morning is good for your body.

(A) glass
(B) glasses
(C) glass of
(D) glasses of

2. _______ you take care of my dog?

(A) Is
(B) Can
(C) Was
(D) Does

Part B. Situational Writing

3.

Samantha is _______ the dog.

(A) petting
(B) walking
(C) washing
(D) carrying

4.

David's friends are not here. David feels _______ today.

(A) angry
(B) happy
(C) lonely
(D) famous

Part C. Practical Reading and Retelling

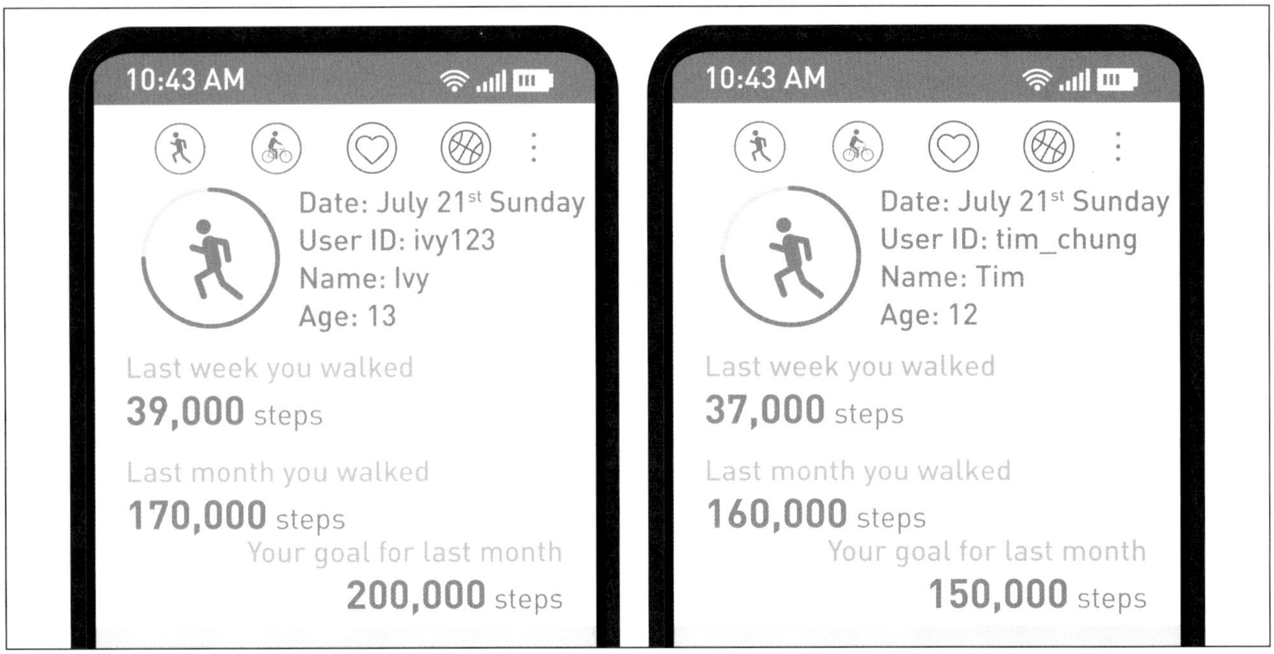

5. What is true about last week?

(A) Ivy walked less than Tim.
(B) Tim walked 40,000 steps.
(C) Tim walked more than Ivy.
(D) Ivy took more than 37,000 steps.

6. What is true about last month?

(A) Tim passed his goal.
(B) Ivy reached her goal.
(C) Tim walked more than Ivy.
(D) Ivy walked 200,000 steps.

Part D. General Reading and Retelling

One Monday morning, Abi's neighbor Mason went to Abi's house. He said, "This is my dog, Thunder. I am going away for one week. Can you take care of Thunder?" Abi looked at Thunder. She did not usually like dogs. But she said, "Sure." After dinner, Abi walked Thunder in the park. He had a lot of energy and tried to smell every tree. He sometimes barked happily at other dogs. Runners in the park noticed Thunder and smiled at him. Children wanted to pet Thunder. That week, Abi walked Thunder every morning and evening. She talked to lots of people in the park. She was never lonely with Thunder. On Saturday, Mason returned from his trip. He went to get Thunder. Abi watched Thunder walk away. She felt sad. She said to Mason, "Thank you for bringing Thunder to me. Life with him was wonderful!"

7. What is the best title for the passage?
   (A) Help Stray Dogs
   (B) Dogs Bring Back Joy
   (C) Strangers are Dangerous
   (D) Sleepy Runners at a Park

8. What is most likely true about Thunder?
   (A) He is lost in the park.
   (B) He is scared of strangers.
   (C) He doesn't like his owner.
   (D) He loves to walk in the park.

9. When did Abi first take Thunder to the park?
   (A) Monday evening
   (B) Tuesday morning
   (C) Wednesday evening
   (D) Saturday morning

10. Why does Abi thank Mason?
    (A) He let her own his dog.
    (B) He returned with a gift.
    (C) His pet made her happy.
    (D) He played games with her.

Listening Practice

Listen and write.

MP3 B2-2

Is Having a Dog Good for You?

One Monday morning, Abi's neighbor Mason went to Abi's house. He said, "This is my dog, Thunder. I am going away for one week. Can you take care of Thunder?" Abi looked at Thunder. She did not usually like dogs. But she said, "Sure." After dinner, Abi walked Thunder in the park. He had a lot of 1 ______ and tried to smell every tree. He sometimes 2 ______ happily at other dogs. Runners in the park 3 ______ Thunder and smiled at him. Children wanted to 4 ______ Thunder. That week, Abi walked Thunder every morning and evening. She talked to lots of people in the park. She was never 5 ______ with Thunder. On Saturday, Mason returned from his trip. He went to get Thunder. Abi watched Thunder walk away. She felt sad. She said to Mason, "Thank you for bringing Thunder to me. Life with him was 6 ______!"

Word Bank

energy	enirgy	baked
fet	wonderfull	pet
lonly	lonely	notict
wonderful	noticed	barked

Listen. Pause. Say each sentence.

MP3 B2-2G

Writing Practice

Write the words.

1 ________

v see

2 ________

adj not happy because you are not with other people

3 ________

v be excited and move around a lot

4 ________

v make the sound of a dog

5 ________

v Is she touching the dog's hair? Then she is ______ting the dog.

6 ________

adj really great

Write the words in each blank.

Summary

Abi's neighbor needed help with his ________________, Thunder. Abi did ________________ like dogs. But she said, "I can ________________ the dog for a week." Abi walked Thunder in the ________________. Abi had fun with Thunder.

Word Puzzle

Complete the word puzzle.

4↓
be excited and move around a lot

2↓
Is she touching the dog's hair? Then she is ______ting the dog.

1↓
really great

3→
see

5→
make the sound of a dog

6→
not happy because you are not with other people

Teacher's Book p.108

UNIT 3

What Is Hay Fever?

Do you have any allergies? If so, which ones?

UNIT 3 What Is Hay Fever?

Luke always carries a pack of tissues in spring and summer. That's because he has hay fever. Hay fever is an allergy. It is called hay fever, but Luke does not have a fever. He has other problems. He gets a runny nose. His eyes water. And he gets headaches. Why does Luke have hay fever every spring and summer? Hay fever comes from grass and trees. The grass and trees have pollen. Pollen is a kind of powder from plants. Luke's body thinks pollen is bad. That's why Luke has these problems. So he does not like playing outside in spring. When he goes out, he wears sunglasses. When he is inside, he closes the windows. He cleans his room often, too. Doing those things helps with the hay fever. But still, Luke gets hay fever every year. When he has bad headaches and a runny nose, he goes to see the doctor. The doctor gives him medicine. The headaches go away for a while. But after a few weeks, they always come back. Hay fever makes Luke sad.

New Words

tissue

n paper for a cold

allergy

n a kind of sickness

your eyes water

you are not crying, but there is water in your eyes

pollen

n a powder from plants

runny nose

n

ex Do you need a tissue?
Maybe you have a runny nose.

go away

v leave

Part A. Sentence Completion

1. Jorge gets a cold _______ winter.

(A) most
(B) many
(C) every
(D) each of

2. Exercise will help me _______ healthy.

(A) stay
(B) stays
(C) is stay
(D) will stay

Part B. Situational Writing

3.

Lia has a bad _______.

(A) cough
(B) headache
(C) runny nose
(D) stomachache

4.

The man is _______.

(A) pulling the door
(B) closing the door
(C) opening the window
(D) cleaning the window

Part C. Practical Reading and Retelling

Spacers for sale!

What is a spacer?

It helps people breathe!

Choose from yellow, red, and blue.

Made by Dr. Tri Mai

Price: $10

Special Event

Get a $2 discount for each spacer!

5. What is true about the spacers?

   (A) There is a green one.

   (B) They help people eat.

   (C) Dr. Tri Mai made them.

   (D) They each cost 12 dollars.

6. How much are two spacers during the special event?

   (A) 14 dollars

   (B) 16 dollars

   (C) 18 dollars

   (D) 20 dollars

Part D. General Reading and Retelling

Luke always carries a pack of tissues in spring and summer. That's because he has hay fever. Hay fever is an allergy. It is called hay fever, but Luke does not have a fever. He has other problems. He gets a runny nose. His eyes water. And he gets headaches. Why does Luke have hay fever every spring and summer? Hay fever comes from grass and trees. The grass and trees have pollen. Pollen is a kind of powder from plants. Luke's body thinks pollen is bad. That's why Luke has these problems. So he does not like playing outside in spring. When he goes out, he wears sunglasses. When he is inside, he closes the windows. He cleans his room often, too. Doing those things helps with the hay fever. But still, Luke gets hay fever every year. When he has bad headaches and a runny nose, he goes to see the doctor. The doctor gives him medicine. The headaches go away for a while. But after a few weeks, they always come back. Hay fever makes Luke sad.

7. What is the best title for the passage?

   (A) Luke's Bad Hay Fever
   (B) Pollen from Different Plants
   (C) Luke's Sunglasses for Hay Fever
   (D) Doctors Stay Away from Hay Fever

8. What is NOT true about hay fever?

   (A) It is from pollen.
   (B) It comes from grass.
   (C) It means having a fever.
   (D) It is common in spring.

9. What does Luke's doctor do?

   (A) get rid of pollen
   (B) give Luke medicine
   (C) cure hay fever perfectly
   (D) clean the hospital every day

10. Why does Luke probably close the windows?

   (A) to take a nap
   (B) to block sunlight
   (C) to wear his sunglasses inside
   (D) to keep pollen out of his room

Listening Practice

Listen and write.

MP3 B2-3

What Is Hay Fever?

Luke always carries a pack of [1] __________ in spring and summer. That's because he has hay fever. Hay fever is an [2] __________. It is called hay fever, but Luke does not have a fever. He has other problems. He gets a runny nose. His eyes [3] __________. And he gets headaches. Why does Luke have hay fever every spring and summer? Hay fever comes from grass and trees. The grass and trees have [4] __________. Pollen is a kind of powder from plants. Luke's body thinks pollen is bad. That's why Luke has these problems. So he does not like playing outside in spring. When he goes out, he wears sunglasses. When he is inside, he closes the windows. He cleans his room often, too. Doing those things helps with the hay fever. But still, Luke gets hay fever every year. When he has bad headaches and a [5] __________, he goes to see the doctor. The doctor gives him medicine. The headaches [6] __________ for a while. But after a few weeks, they always come back. Hay fever makes Luke sad.

Word Bank

runny nose	runnynose	go eway
go away	tissues	allergy
allergie	water	pollen
wader	tisues	pallen

Listen. Pause. Say each sentence.

MP3 B2-3G

Writing Practice

Write the words.

1 ____________________

n paper for a cold

2 ____________________

n a kind of sickness

3 ____________________

you are not crying, but there is water in your eyes

4 ____________________

n a powder from plants

5 ____________________

n

ex Do you need a tissue?
Maybe you have a _______.

6 ____________________

v leave

Write the words in each blank.

Summary

Luke has hay fever. Hay fever comes from ____________________ and trees. In the spring and ____________________, Luke always carries ____________________. He closes the ____________________ and stays inside. Hay fever makes Luke sad.

Word Puzzle

Complete the word puzzle.

1↓
a powder from plants

2↓
leave

4↓
paper for a cold

3↓
you are not crying, but there is water in your eyes

5→
Do you need a tissue? Maybe you have a _______.

6→
a kind of sickness

Teacher's Book
p.112

UNIT 4

Smartphone Posture

Do you use a smartphone?
If so, do you look down or up at it?

UNIT 4 Smartphone Posture

Do you use your smartphone a lot? Do you look down at your phone? Does your neck hurt? Did you say "yes" to all the questions? Then you are in trouble! That's because your head can hurt your spine. What is your spine? It is the bones in your back. Hurting your spine is not a good idea. It will cause neck and back problems. Sadly, many students use their phone four hours a day. They hurt their spine for four hours every day. How can we stop this? Here is some advice from experts. First, do not look down at your phone. Hold it up! Your arms will hurt, but this is great exercise! Second, lie on the floor. Then, hold up the phone. But be careful! Don't drop your phone! You might hurt your nose. Third, use your voice. Speak your messages and emails. Then you do not have to look down. Finally, stretch after you use your phone. This can help your spine. Follow the advice of experts. Remember: you only get one spine.

New Words

look down at

v point your head down and look

in trouble

adj having problems

spine

n the bones of your back

advice

n useful information

expert

n

ex Does she know a lot about cars? Then she is an expert on cars.

stretch

v reach out as exercise

Part A. Sentence Completion

1. Here _______ some advice.

(A) is
(B) do
(C) be
(D) does

2. Not enough sleep might _______ you sick.

(A) make
(B) made
(C) will make
(D) have make

Part B. Situational Writing

3.

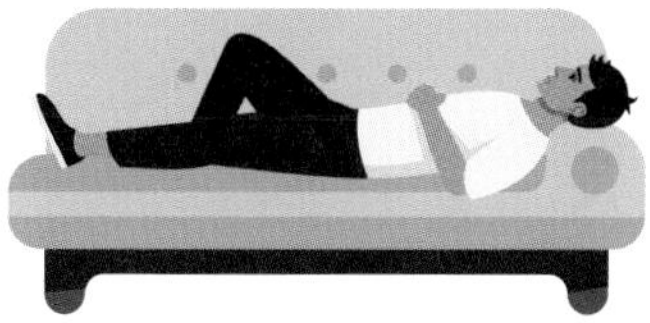

He is _______ on the sofa.

(A) lying
(B) sitting
(C) eating
(D) standing

4.

Don't hurt your _______!

(A) lung
(B) wrist
(C) heart
(D) spine

Part C. Practical Reading and Retelling

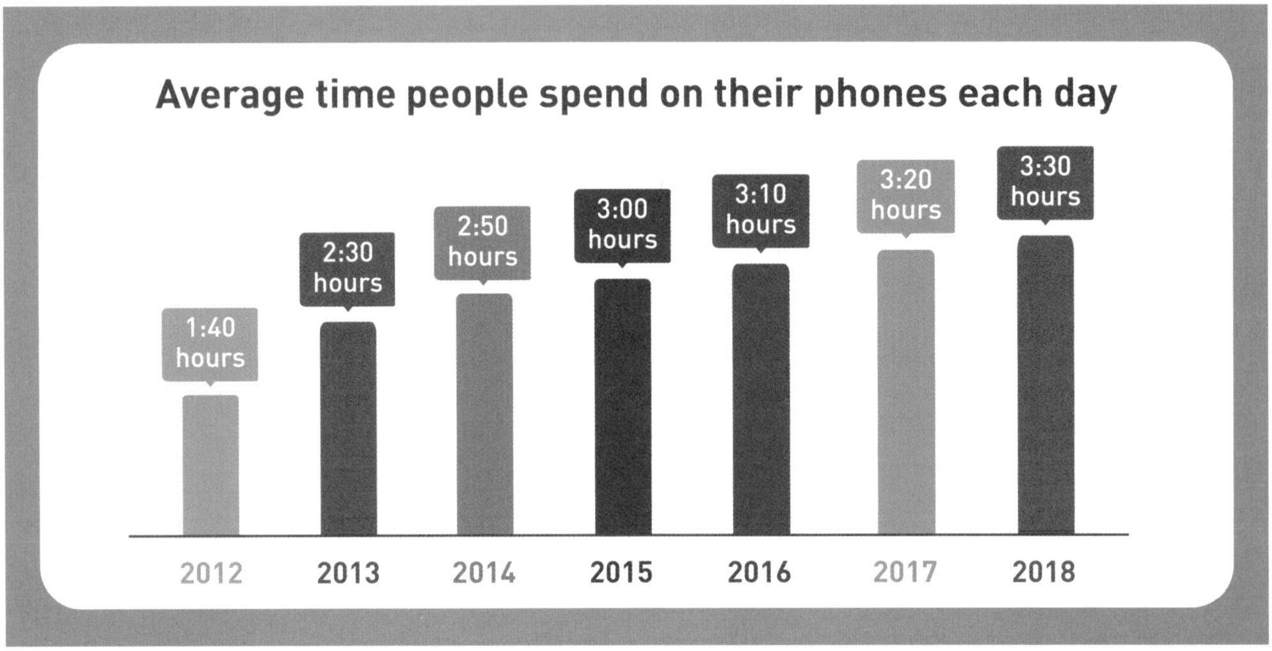

5. On average, when did people use their phones the most?

(A) in 2012

(B) in 2014

(C) in 2015

(D) in 2018

6. On average, how many hours did people use their phones in 2014?

(A) 2 hours and 30 minutes

(B) 2 hours and 50 minutes

(C) 3 hours and 10 minutes

(D) 3 hours and 20 minutes

Part D. General Reading and Retelling

Do you use your smartphone a lot? Do you look down at your phone? Does your neck hurt? Did you say "yes" to all the questions? Then you are in trouble! That's because your head can hurt your spine. What is your spine? It is the bones in your back. Hurting your spine is not a good idea. It will cause neck and back problems. Sadly, many students use their phone four hours a day. They hurt their spine for four hours every day. How can we stop this? Here is some advice from experts. First, do not look down at your phone. Hold it up! Your arms will hurt, but this is great exercise! Second, lie on the floor. Then, hold up the phone. But be careful! Don't drop your phone! <u>You might hurt your nose</u>. Third, use your voice. Speak your messages and emails. Then you do not have to look down. Finally, stretch after you use your phone. This can help your spine. Follow the advice of experts. Remember: you only get one spine.

7. What is the best title for the passage?
   - (A) How to Buy a Better Phone
   - (B) Your Eyes Hurt from Using Phones
   - (C) Don't Drop Your Phone in the Street
   - (D) Stop Hurting Your Spine with Phones

8. According to the passage, why do smartphone users get neck problems?
   - (A) Their eyes look up.
   - (B) Their phone is too big.
   - (C) Their head hurts their spine.
   - (D) Their phone makes loud sounds.

9. Which is a tip in the passage?
   - (A) wearing glasses
   - (B) lying on the floor
   - (C) sitting in a low chair
   - (D) buying a smaller phone

10. Why does the passage say, "You might hurt your nose"?
   - (A) Walking can be dangerous.
   - (B) You might fall off your bike.
   - (C) You might drop your phone.
   - (D) Playing baseball can be dangerous.

Listening Practice

Listen and write.

MP3 B2-4

Smartphone Posture

Do you use your smartphone a lot? Do you [1] ____ your phone? Does your neck hurt? Did you say “yes” to all the questions? Then you are [2] ____! That’s because your head can hurt your [3] ____. What is your spine? It is the bones in your back. Hurting your spine is not a good idea. It will cause neck and back problems. Sadly, many students use their phone four hours a day. They hurt their spine for four hours every day. How can we stop this? Here is some [4] ____ from [5] ____. First, do not look down at your phone. Hold it up! Your arms will hurt, but this is great exercise! Second, lie on the floor. Then, hold up the phone. But be careful! Don’t drop your phone! You might hurt your nose. Third, use your voice. Speak your messages and emails. Then you do not have to look down. Finally, [6] ____ after you use your phone. This can help your spine. Follow the advice of experts. Remember: you only get one spine.

Word Bank

spin	in trouble	experts
expurts	look down at	stretch
and trouble	adbice	lookdownat
stretcch	advice	spine

Listen. Pause. Say each sentence.

MP3 B2-4G

Writing Practice

Write the words.

1 ________________ *v* point your head down and look	2 ________________ *adj* having problems
3 ________________ *n* the bones of your back 	4 ________________ *n* useful information
5 ________________ *n* ex Does she know a lot about cars? Then she is an _______ on cars.	6 ________________ *v* reach out as exercise

Write the words in each blank.

Summary

Do not look ________________ at your phone. It can hurt your ________________. Instead, hold ________________ the phone. Also, lie down. You can use your voice, too. Finally, ________________ after you use your phone!

Word Puzzle

Complete the word puzzle.

1 → having problems

2 ↓ point your head down and look

3 → useful information

4 ↓ reach out as exercise

6 → Does she know a lot about cars? Then she is an _______ on cars.

5 ↓ the bones of your back

The Greedy Fox

Teacher's Book p.116

A fox had a long winter and was very hungry. He looked around for some food. Finally, he found a tree with a hole in it. Inside the hole, there was food! It was a family's picnic. There were three sandwiches, a bowl of rice, some soup, an apple, an orange, two cookies, two brownies, some cake, some juice, and some cola. The fox climbed inside the hole. He started to eat the food. The fox ate the first sandwich. It was a meat sandwich, and it was delicious. Then he ate the peanut butter sandwich. At that point, the fox was full. But the food was so delicious. He kept eating anyway. He ate the rice, the soup, the fruit, and the dessert. He drank the juice and the cola. Soon, his stomach was huge. The fox wanted to go home to take a nap. He started to leave the hole. But when he tried, he soon learned he was stuck. He remembered a lesson from his parents: When you are full, stop eating.

CHAPTER 2

Food Trend

Teacher's Book
p.117

UNIT 5

Hawaiian Pizza

What is your favorite kind of pizza?

UNIT 5 Hawaiian Pizza

What is the most famous Hawaiian invention? Some people might say it is Hawaiian pizza. However, Hawaiian pizza is not from Hawaii. The inventor of Hawaiian pizza was not Hawaiian. He was not Italian, either. So where did it come from? In 1962, Sam Panopoulos made the first Hawaiian pizza in Ontario, Canada. His Hawaiian pizza had ham, cheese, and pineapple. People say he was first to put pineapple on a pizza. Panopoulos and his brothers tasted the pizza. The pizza was sweet and salty at the same time! The pineapple was very juicy. Why did he call it Hawaiian pizza? The secret is on a can of pineapple slices. The brand name on the can was Hawaii, so he named it Hawaiian pizza. Today, people call pizza with pineapple Hawaiian. Usually, the pineapple is from a can. Some people love it, but some people don't. Actually, some people hate it. A famous cook called Gordon Ramsay is one of them. He said pineapple should never be on a pizza.

New Words

invention *n* new creation	**Hawaiian** *adj* from Hawaii, a sunny island in the U.S.
inventor *n* ex Did he create something new? Then he is an <u>inventor</u>.	**taste** *v* try a food
can *n* round metal with food in it 	**slice** *n* a piece

Part A. Sentence Completion

1. Benz invented the world's _______ automobile.

(A) a
(B) an
(C) one
(D) first

2. My favorite pizza toppings are ham, tomatoes, _______ mushrooms.

(A) so
(B) and
(C) and is
(D) they are

Part B. Situational Writing

3.

The cook is _______ the soup.

(A) tasting
(B) mixing
(C) ordering
(D) delivering

4.

Ken made a new _______. It can fly.

(A) bird
(B) ball
(C) insect
(D) invention

Part C. Practical Reading and Retelling

Make Hawaiian pizza with your dad!

This is a cooking class for two people - one adult and one child.

- Place: Manuel's Pizza Shop
- Time / Date: 3 PM October 3rd
- Fee: $ 10 for two people

Only 30 people can make pizza at this event! Join now!

5. Kareem wants to make pizza with his dad, with Luna, and with Luna's dad. How much will it cost in total?

(A) 5 dollars

(B) 10 dollars

(C) 15 dollars

(D) 20 dollars

6. When is this event?

(A) at 10 AM

(B) at 2 PM

(C) in October

(D) on November 3rd

Part D. General Reading and Retelling

What is the most famous Hawaiian invention? Some people might say it is Hawaiian pizza. However, Hawaiian pizza is not from Hawaii. The inventor of Hawaiian pizza was not Hawaiian. He was not Italian, either. So where did it come from? In 1962, Sam Panopoulos made the first Hawaiian pizza in Ontario, Canada. His Hawaiian pizza had ham, cheese, and pineapple. People say he was first to put pineapple on a pizza. Panopoulos and his brothers tasted the pizza. The pizza was sweet and salty at the same time! The pineapple was very juicy. Why did he call it Hawaiian pizza? The secret is on a can of pineapple slices. The brand name on the can was Hawaii, so he named it Hawaiian pizza. Today, people call pizza with pineapple Hawaiian. Usually, the pineapple is from a can. Some people love it, but some people don't. Actually, some people ________ it. A famous cook called Gordon Ramsay is one of them. He said pineapple should never be on a pizza.

7. What is the main idea of the passage?
   (A) Italy is the best place for pizza.
   (B) Gordon Ramsay loves pineapples.
   (C) Hawaiian pizza is not from Hawaii.
   (D) Panopoulos makes the best pizza.

8. According to the passage, where did Panopoulos make the first Hawaiian pizza?
   (A) in Italy
   (B) in Korea
   (C) in Hawaii
   (D) in Canada

9. According to the passage, why did Panopoulos name the pizza "Hawaiian"?
   (A) He came from Hawaii.
   (B) The pizza looked like Hawaii.
   (C) Hawaii was his favorite place.
   (D) It was the name on a can of pineapple.

10. Which word is best for the blank?
   (A) eat
   (B) like
   (C) hate
   (D) touch

Listening Practice

Listen and write.

MP3 B2-5

Hawaiian Pizza

What is the most famous Hawaiian [1] ______? Some people might say it is [2] ______ pizza. However, Hawaiian pizza is not from Hawaii. The [3] ______ of Hawaiian pizza was not Hawaiian. He was not Italian, either. So where did it come from? In 1962, Sam Panopoulos made the first Hawaiian pizza in Ontario, Canada. His Hawaiian pizza had ham, cheese, and pineapple. People say he was first to put pineapple on a pizza. Panopoulos and his brothers [4] ______ the pizza. The pizza was sweet and salty at the same time! The pineapple was very juicy. Why did he call it Hawaiian pizza? The secret is on a can of pineapple [5] ______. The brand name on the can was Hawaii, so he named it Hawaiian pizza. Today, people call pizza with pineapple Hawaiian. Usually, the pineapple is from a [6] ______. Some people love it, but some people don't. Actually, some people hate it. A famous cook called Gordon Ramsay is one of them. He said pineapple should never be on a pizza.

Word Bank

inventor	enventor	slice
can	Fawaiian	slices
invenshion	tasted	taste
invention	kan	Hawaiian

Listen. Pause. Say each sentence.

MP3 B2-5G

Writing Practice

Write the words.

1 ______________ *n* new creation	2 ______________ *adj* from Hawaii, a sunny island in the U.S.
3 ______________ *n* ex Did he create something new? Then he is an ______.	4 ______________ *v* try a food
5 ______________ *n* round metal with food in it 	6 ______________ *n* a piece

Write the words in each blank.

Summary

The ______________ of Hawaiian pizza was a Canadian. He thought ______________ on pizza was delicious. It had a ______________ and salty taste. But some people do not ______________ Hawaiian pizza.

Word Puzzle

Complete the word puzzle.

1 ↓
try a food

2 →
a piece

3 →
Did he create something new? Then he is an ______.

3 ↓
new creation

4 →
round metal with food in it

5 →
from Hawaii, a sunny island in the U.S.

Teacher's Book
p.121

UNIT 6

Fourth Meal

How many meals do you eat each day?
Do you have snacks between meals?

UNIT 6 Fourth Meal

Many people eat three meals a day: breakfast, lunch, and dinner. But in some countries, people eat more meals. Some people in Poland have a second breakfast. And many people in England have an afternoon snack. These meals are called a "fourth meal." Many people now enjoy fourth meals. But these meals are not always healthy. That's why some countries are worried about people's health. Richard Mattes is a professor at Purdue University. He studies people's meals. Mattes says one fourth meal is usually about 580 calories. But it should only be about 200 calories. Yogurt, fruit, almonds, vegetables, and milk are good choices. However, most people do not eat these healthy foods. They like to eat fast food as a fourth meal. They eat burgers, pizza, tacos, and fried chicken. It is easy to buy fast food. Many fast food restaurants are open 24 hours every day. Also, these foods are often delicious. However, a healthy fourth meal is a better idea.

New Words

meal

n breakfast, lunch, or dinner

calorie

n energy from food

snack

n food between breakfast, lunch, or dinner

taco

n a Mexican food

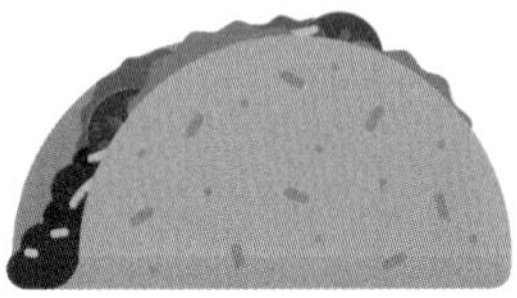

fast food

n

ex Was the restaurant food ready in one minute? Maybe it is fast food.

healthy

adj good for your body's health

10 minutes

Part A. Sentence Completion

1. _______ many calories are we eating with this meal?

(A) Who
(B) How
(C) What
(D) Where

2. A mouse _______ small.

(A) usually
(B) is usually
(C) usually be
(D) are usually

Part B. Situational Writing

3.

Wilbur likes to eat _______.

(A) fast food
(B) vegetables
(C) healthy food
(D) tomato salads

4.

Lily won the _______ prize.

(A) first
(B) second
(C) third
(D) fourth

Part C. Practical Reading and Retelling

5. Where is the pizza place?

   (A) right behind the cafe
   (B) in front of the library
   (C) under the ice cream shop
   (D) next to the taco restaurant

6. Which two shops are in the same building?

   (A) the cafe and the pizza place
   (B) the cafe and the ice cream shop
   (C) the salad cafe and the burger shop
   (D) the pizza place and the taco restaurant

Part D. General Reading and Retelling

Many people eat three meals a day: breakfast, lunch, and dinner. But in some countries, people eat more meals. Some people in Poland have a second breakfast. And many people in England have an afternoon snack. These meals are called a "fourth meal." Many people now enjoy fourth meals. But these meals are not always healthy. That's why some countries are __________ about people's health. Richard Mattes is a professor at Purdue University. He studies people's meals. Mattes says one fourth meal is usually about 580 calories. But it should only be about 200 calories. Yogurt, fruit, almonds, vegetables, and milk are good choices. However, most people do not eat these healthy foods. They like to eat fast food as a fourth meal. They eat burgers, pizza, tacos, and fried chicken. It is easy to buy fast food. Many fast food restaurants are open 24 hours every day. Also, these foods are often delicious. However, a healthy fourth meal is a better idea.

7. Why did the author write this passage?
   (A) to ask about online food
   (B) to tell people about a fourth meal
   (C) to ask when people eat breakfast
   (D) to explain about the calories in fast food

8. According to the passage, what is NOT a healthy fourth meal?
   (A) fruit
   (B) yogurt
   (C) burgers
   (D) vegetables

9. According to the passage, when is most likely the fourth meal in England?
   (A) at 11 AM
   (B) at noon
   (C) at 4 PM
   (D) at midnight

10. Which word is best for the blank?
   (A) glad
   (B) tired
   (C) happy
   (D) worried

Listening Practice

Listen and write.

MP3 B2-6

Fourth Meal

Many people eat three [1] ____________ a day: breakfast, lunch, and dinner. But in some countries, people eat more meals. Some people in Poland have a second breakfast. And many people in England have an afternoon [2] ____________. These meals are called a "fourth meal." Many people now enjoy fourth meals. But these meals are not always [3] ____________. That's why some countries are worried about people's health. Richard Mattes is a professor at Purdue University. He studies people's meals. Mattes says one fourth meal is usually about 580 [4] ____________. But it should only be about 200 calories. Yogurt, fruit, almonds, vegetables, and milk are good choices. However, most people do not eat these healthy foods. They like to eat [5] ____________ as a fourth meal. They eat burgers, pizza, [6] ____________, and fried chicken. It is easy to buy fast food. Many fast food restaurants are open 24 hours every day. Also, these foods are often delicious. However, a healthy fourth meal is a better idea.

Word Bank

snack	calories	helthy
meals	sneck	healthy
callories	fast food	mills
taccos	past food	tacos

Listen. Pause. Say each sentence.

MP3 B2-6G

Writing Practice

Write the words.

1 ________ *n* breakfast, lunch, or dinner	2 ________ *n* energy from food
3 ________ *n* food between breakfast, lunch, or dinner	4 ________ *n* a Mexican food 
5 ________ *n* ex Was the restaurant food ready in one minute? Maybe it is ______.	6 ________ *adj* good for your body's health

Write the words in each blank.

Summary

In some countries, people eat a "fourth ________". However, a fourth meal is ________ always healthy. Many people eat fast ________. Instead, they should choose to eat a ________ fourth meal.

Word Puzzle

Complete the word puzzle.

1↓
Was the restaurant food ready in one minute? Maybe it is _______.

3↓
energy from food

2↓
good for your body's health

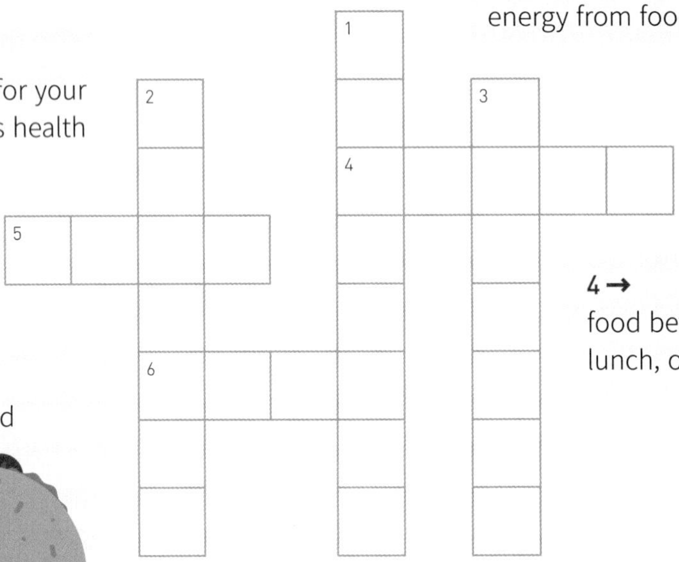

5→
breakfast, lunch, or dinner

4→
food between breakfast, lunch, or dinner

6→
a Mexican food

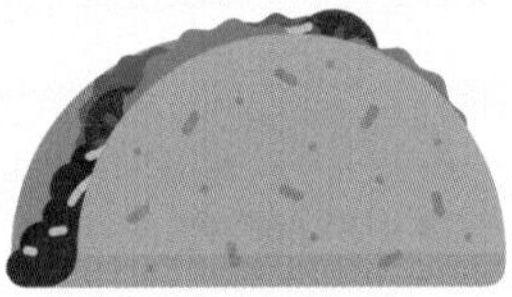

Teacher's Book p.125

UNIT 7

Jamie and Local Food

Is there a famous vegetable or fruit from your town?
What is it?

UNIT 7 Jamie and Local Food

Jamie went to a supermarket with his mom. He picked up an onion. A sign near the onion said, "Local Food." It also had a picture of a farmer on it. The farmer's name was Dario Bonifaz. Jamie asked Tommy about local food. Tommy is a worker at the supermarket. Tommy said, "Local food is healthy and fresh. That's because local food comes from a nearby place. It is very delicious because it doesn't travel a long time on a truck. Plus, you know who grows it!" Tommy also said, "Jamie, you can grow local food at home." Jamie was excited! He came home and asked his mom about local food. He wanted to grow plants for food in his house. Jamie's mom gave him a box with dirt. He put tomato seeds in it. Then, he watered his tomato seeds. After that, he put a light over them. His tomato plants started growing. At that point, he put them under sunlight. Eighty days later, he had delicious red tomatoes! He ate them with his family.

New Words

local

adj from your town

fresh

adj not cooked and not old

dirt

n

ex Do you want your seed to grow? Put it in dirt.

truck

n

ex How can we carry many boxes? We can use a truck.

at that point

adv then

seed

n a small part of a plant before it grows

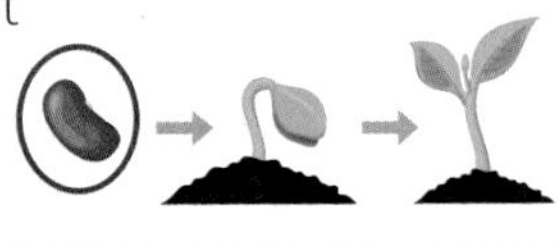

Part A. Sentence Completion

1. _______ made this sandwich?

(A) How
(B) Who
(C) Why
(D) Where

2. Jamie's mom gave _______ a box with dirt.

(A) he
(B) his
(C) him
(D) he's

Part B. Situational Writing

3.

Asma is _______flowers.

(A) cutting
(B) picking
(C) planting
(D) watering

4.

The box is _______.

(A) closed tightly
(B) filled with toys
(C) under the guitar
(D) behind the teddy bear

Part C. Practical Reading and Retelling

5. What is the first step?
   (A) picking fruit
   (B) planting seeds
   (C) watering the plants
   (D) putting light on the plants

6. What does Jamie do right after he first puts the plants in open sunlight?
   (A) eats the tomatoes
   (B) plants more seeds
   (C) picks the tomatoes
   (D) waters the plants again

Part D. General Reading and Retelling

Jamie went to a supermarket with his mom. He picked up an onion. A sign near the onion said, "Local Food." It also had a picture of a farmer on it. The farmer's name was Dario Bonifaz. Jamie asked Tommy about local food. Tommy is a worker at the supermarket. Tommy said, "Local food is healthy and fresh. That's because local food comes from a ________ place. It is very delicious because it doesn't travel a long time on a truck. Plus, you know who grows it!" Tommy also said, "Jamie, you can grow local food at home." Jamie was excited! He came home and asked his mom about local food. He wanted to grow plants for food in his house. Jamie's mom gave him a box with dirt. He put tomato seeds in it. Then, he watered his tomato seeds. After that, he put a light over them. His tomato plants started growing. At that point, he put them under sunlight. Eighty days later, he had delicious red tomatoes! He ate them with his family.

7. What is the main idea of the passage?

(A) Jamie watered his onions.
(B) Dario has the best tomatoes.
(C) Tomatoes grew after 80 days.
(D) Jamie learned about local food.

8. According to the passage, who is Dario?

(A) a kid shopping
(B) a tomato seller
(C) a farmer of onions
(D) a worker at the supermarket

9. What did Jamie do first after he watered the seeds?

(A) dig a hole
(B) put a light over them
(C) eat them with his family
(D) put the box under sunlight

10. Which word is best for the blank?

(A) dirty
(B) messy
(C) nearby
(D) faraway

Listening Practice

Listen and write.

MP3 B2-7

Jamie and Local Food

Jamie went to a supermarket with his mom. He picked up an onion. A sign near the onion said, “Local Food.” It also had a picture of a farmer on it. The farmer’s name was Dario Bonifaz. Jamie asked Tommy about [1] food. Tommy is a worker at the supermarket. Tommy said, “Local food is healthy and [2] . That’s because local food comes from a nearby place. It is very delicious because it doesn’t travel a long time on a [3] . Plus, you know who grows it!” Tommy also said, “Jamie, you can grow local food at home.” Jamie was excited! He came home and asked his mom about local food. He wanted to grow plants for food in his house. Jamie’s mom gave him a box with [4] . He put tomato [5] in it. Then, he watered his tomato seeds. After that, he put a light over them. His tomato plants started growing. [6] , he put them under sunlight. Eighty days later, he had delicious red tomatoes! He ate them with his family.

Word Bank

fresh	rocal	seeds
Athatpoint	local	dirt
frash	truck	trukk
dert	At that point	sids

Listen. Pause. Say each sentence.

MP3 B2-7G

Writing Practice

Write the words.

1 ____________________

adj from your town

2 ____________________

adj not cooked and not old

3 ____________________

n

ex Do you want your seed to grow? Put it in ______.

4 ____________________

n

ex How can we carry many boxes? We can use a ______.

5 ____________________

adv then

6 ____________________

n a small part of a plant before it grows

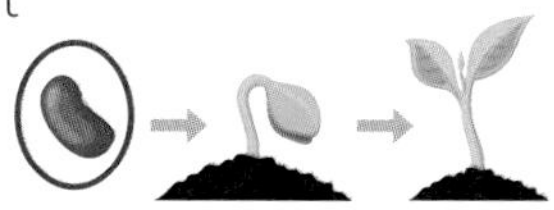

Write the words in each blank.

Summary

Jamie asked Tommy about ________________ food at a supermarket. Tommy ________________ local food was healthy. He said Jamie could ________________ his own food. Jame grew some ________________ at home.

Word Puzzle

Complete the word puzzle.

1 →
not cooked and not old

2 ↓
a small part of a plant before it grows

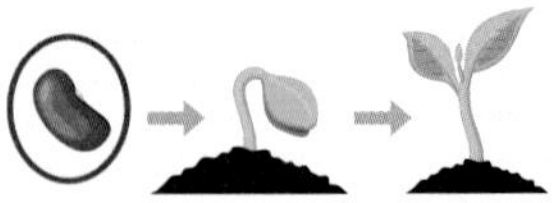

3 ↓
then

4 →
Do you want your seed to grow? Put it in ______.

5 →
How can we carry many boxes? We can use a ______.

6 →
from your town

Teacher's Book p.129

UNIT 8

Good Avocados

Do you like avocados? Why or why not?

UNIT 8 Good Avocados

Avocados are popular fruit. But how can you choose a good avocado? And how can you eat one? First, remember that some avocados do not taste good. That's because sometimes they are not ripe yet. To be ripe means to be ready to eat. So when are avocados ripe? Remember to check the color and to feel each avocado. Bright green avocados are not ripe yet. They feel very hard, too. If you buy a bright green or hard avocado, don't eat it for 4 to 5 days. The color of a perfect avocado is dark green. It can even be purple. And it feels soft, but not too soft. A very soft avocado is overripe. That means it is past being ripe. It will not taste great anymore. The color of an overripe avocado is brown or yellow. Next, you must cut the avocado. How do you cut an avocado? Cut it in half, and take out the seed in the middle. Then, scoop out the avocado with a spoon. Now you can make a delicious avocado smoothie or salad!

New Words

avocado
n a soft green fruit

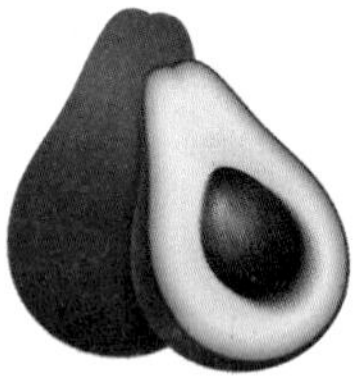

ripe
adj ready to eat

hard
adj not soft

overripe
adj too ripe

cut X in half
v cut X in its middle part

scoop out
v take out with a spoon

Part A. Sentence Completion

1. This tomato _______ taste good. It is not ripe.

(A) no
(B) don't
(C) doesn't
(D) don't not

2. A good apple is hard, _______ not too hard.

(A) as
(B) for
(C) but
(D) than

Part B. Situational Writing

3.

Get a bucket and _______ some sand.

(A) pull
(B) carry
(C) throw
(D) scoop out

4.

The banana on the right is _______.

(A) green
(B) sliced
(C) overripe
(D) chopped

Busker Cafe

Order sheet for:
October 2020

#	Items	Price for 1	Number of items
1	a bag of oranges	$2	10
2	a bag of lemons	$1	5
3	a bag of avocados	$2	10
4	a pack of blueberries	$4	5
5	a pack of strawberries	$5	4

5. How many packs of strawberries does Busker Cafe buy?

(A) 4
(B) 5
(C) 10
(D) 30

6. How much does Busker Cafe pay for avocados in total?

(A) 5 dollars
(B) 10 dollars
(C) 15 dollars
(D) 20 dollars

Part D. General Reading and Retelling

Avocados are popular fruit. But how can you choose a good avocado? And how can you eat one? First, remember that some avocados do not taste good. That's because sometimes they are not ripe yet. To be ripe means to be ready to eat. So when are avocados ripe? Remember to check the color and to feel each avocado. Bright green avocados are not ripe yet. They feel very hard, too. If you buy a bright green or hard avocado, don't eat it for 4 to 5 days. The color of a perfect avocado is dark green. It can even be purple. And it feels soft, but not too soft. A very soft avocado is overripe. That means it is past being ripe. It will not taste great anymore. The color of an overripe avocado is brown or yellow. Next, you must cut the avocado. How do you cut an avocado? Cut it in half, and take out the seed in the middle. Then, scoop out the avocado with a spoon. Now you can make a delicious avocado smoothie or salad!

7. What is the best title for the passage?
   - (A) Why Avocados Are Healthy
   - (B) Coloring Avocados in Art Class
   - (C) How to Choose a Good Avocado
   - (D) How to Make an Avocado Smoothie

8. According to the passage, what color is a good avocado?
   - (A) yellow
   - (B) brown
   - (C) dark green
   - (D) bright green

9. According to the passage, what is true about avocados?
   - (A) They are always green.
   - (B) Avocados are not popular.
   - (C) Hard avocados taste good.
   - (D) There is a seed in the middle.

10. Which avocado would be best after 4 days?
   - (A) a hard avocado
   - (B) a yellow avocado
   - (C) a very soft avocado
   - (D) an avocado without a seed

Listening Practice

Listen and write.

MP3 B2-8

Good Avocados

Avocados are popular fruit. But how can you choose a good 1 ____________ ? And how can you eat one? First, remember that some avocados do not taste good. That's because sometimes they are not 2 ____________ yet. To be ripe means to be ready to eat. So when are avocados ripe? Remember to check the color and to feel each avocado. Bright green avocados are not ripe yet. They feel very 3 ____________ , too. If you buy a bright green or hard avocado, don't eat it for 4 to 5 days. The color of a perfect avocado is dark green. It can even be purple. And it feels soft, but not too soft. A very soft avocado is 4 ____________ . That means it is past being ripe. It will not taste great anymore. The color of an overripe avocado is brown or yellow. Next, you must cut the avocado. How do you cut an avocado? Cut it 5 ____________ , and take out the seed in the middle. Then, 6 ____________ out the avocado with a spoon. Now you can make a delicious avocado smoothie or salad!

Word Bank

ripe	overripe	abocado
inhalf	avocado	scoup
hod	in half	lipe
hard	scoop	overrip

Listen. Pause. Say each sentence.

MP3 B2-8G

Writing Practice

Write the words.

1 ________ *n* a soft green fruit 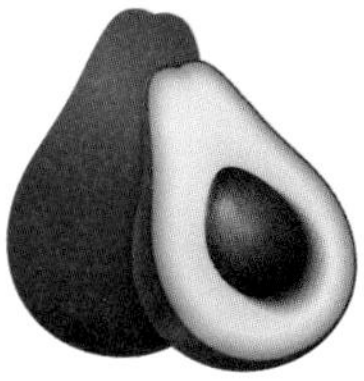	2 ________ *adj* ready to eat
3 ________ *adj* not soft	4 ________ *adj* too ripe
cut X 5 ________ *v* cut X in its middle part	6 ________ *v* take out with a spoon

Write the words in each blank.

Summary

Are you buying an avocado? Check the ________ and feel each avocado. Are you eating an avocado? Cut the avocado in ________ and take out the ________. ________ out the avocado.

Word Puzzle

Complete the word puzzle.

1↓
a soft green fruit

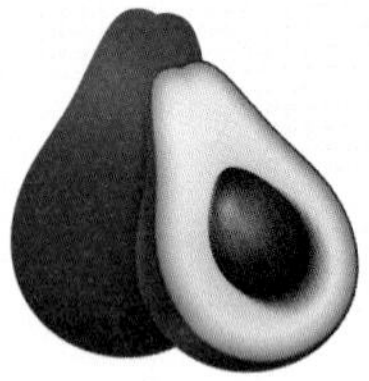

2→
take out with a spoon

3↓
too ripe

4→
not soft

5→
cut X in its middle part

6→
ready to eat

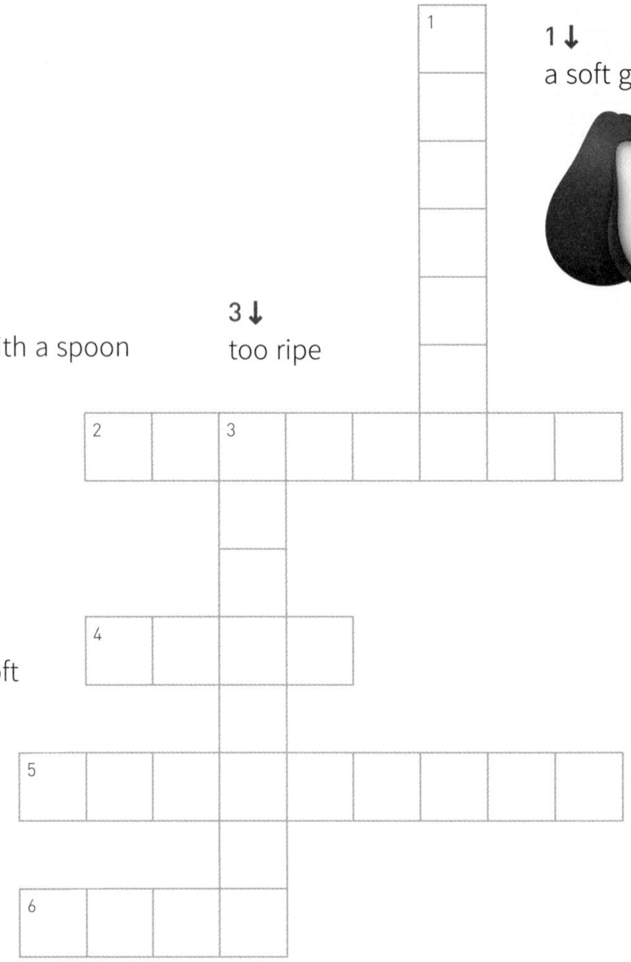

CHAPTER REVIEW

What is it?

Teacher's Book p.133

My class is doing a project on fruit. Our teacher asked us to write a speech and make a costume of our favorite fruit. First, I read about my fruit on the internet. It grows best in hot places. You must be careful when you touch the outside. You might cut your hand. Many different countries grow and eat the fruit. It is also common to drink its juice. I like to eat it with ham on pizza. For my costume, I wear a big yellow shirt and big yellow pants. I fill them with cotton until I am big and round. Then, I make a hat with long, green leaves. I stand up in front of the class and do my speech about my fruit. My teacher likes my speech and gives me an "A." My mother and father are very proud.

CHAPTER 3

Arts and Crafts

Teacher's Book p.134

UNIT 9

Art Gallery of Saint Peter

Do you like visiting art galleries?
What kind of art do you enjoy?

UNIT 9 Art Gallery of Saint Peter

The Art Gallery of Saint Peter welcomes everyone! We are open from 10 AM to 5 PM Monday to Sunday! But on Wednesdays, we are open until 9 PM. The tickets are 15 dollars for adults, and 10 dollars for students. Children under 5 get in for free. On Wednesday nights, from 6 PM to 9 PM, entry is free for everyone. That is called Art Wednesday Nights. We have more than 90,000 artworks in our gallery. The works are from Africa, America, Asia, and Europe. Please remember, you cannot take pictures! There is a special artwork section, too. Right now that section is showing Rebecca Neilstein's artworks. It ends on May 8th, 2019. The art in the special section changes every 6 months. Do you need a tour of the gallery? There are five tours every day, from 11 AM to 4 PM. There is one tour every hour. One tour takes about 40 minutes. The tours are always free! For more information about the Art Gallery of Saint Peter, visit our website at www.saintpeterart.org.

New Words

open until ex Is the store open until 9 PM? Then it closes its doors at 9 PM.	**entry** *n* going in
artwork *n* a piece of art	**section** *n* area
for more information about to learn more about	**website** *n* page on the internet

10 minutes

Part A. Sentence Completion

1. The store is open from 9 AM _______ 10 PM.

(A) to
(B) at
(C) on
(D) for

2. We have _______ than twenty students in our art club!

(A) as
(B) over
(C) more
(D) more as

Part B. Situational Writing

3.

There are three _______ in the art gallery.

(A) walls
(B) adults
(C) children
(D) sections

4.

The woman with the red flag is a _______.

(A) driver
(B) tour guide
(C) store owner
(D) photographer

Art Gallery of Saint Peter

NOW we have:

3rd Floor	Special Section Rebecca Neilstein's works
2nd Floor	Artworks from Africa
1st Floor	Artworks from Europe

Please pay $10 more at the door for the special section.

5. Where are the museum's artworks from Europe?

(A) on the first floor
(B) on the second floor
(C) on the third floor
(D) The museum has no artworks from Europe.

6. According to the map, what should you do before you go to the third floor?

(A) wash your hands
(B) pay $10 at the door
(C) turn off your cell phone
(D) learn about Rebecca Neilstein

Part D. General Reading and Retelling

The Art Gallery of Saint Peter welcomes everyone! We are open from 10 AM to 5 PM Monday to Sunday! But on Wednesdays, we are open until 9 PM. The tickets are 15 dollars for adults, and 10 dollars for students. Children under 5 get in for free. On Wednesday nights, from 6 PM to 9 PM, entry is free for everyone. That is called Art Wednesday Nights. We have more than 90,000 artworks in our gallery. The works are from Africa, America, Asia, and Europe. Please remember, you cannot take pictures! There is a special artwork section, too. Right now that section is showing Rebecca Neilstein's artworks. It ends on May 8th, 2019. The art in the special section changes every 6 months. Do you need a tour of the gallery? There are five tours every day, from 11 AM to 4 PM. There is one tour every hour. One tour takes about 40 minutes. The tours are always free! For more information about the Art Gallery of Saint Peter, visit our website at www.saintpeterart.org.

7. What is the best title for the passage?
   - (A) Art Gallery Programs for Kids
   - (B) Join Art Wednesday Nights for Free
   - (C) We Need Volunteers for Gallery Tours
   - (D) Welcome to the Art Gallery of Saint Peter

8. According to the passage, what is true about the Art Gallery of Saint Peter?
   - (A) A tour takes about 40 minutes.
   - (B) It is open until 9 PM on Mondays.
   - (C) It has fewer than 80,000 artworks.
   - (D) The special section changes every month.

9. According to the passage, what happens on Art Wednesday Nights?
   - (A) The art gallery is free.
   - (B) There is a party at the gallery.
   - (C) The gallery is open until 10 PM.
   - (D) Children cannot go to the art gallery.

10. What can you probably NOT see in the art gallery?
   - (A) ten people on a gallery tour at 2 PM
   - (B) two women looking at an African artwork
   - (C) a boy taking pictures of Neilstein's works
   - (D) two adults paying 30 dollars to enter on Tuesday

Listening Practice

Listen and write.

MP3 B2-9

Art Gallery of Saint Peter

The Art Gallery of Saint Peter welcomes everyone! We are open from 10 AM to 5 PM Monday to Sunday! But on Wednesdays, we are [1] ______________ 9 PM. The tickets are 15 dollars for adults, and 10 dollars for students. Children under 5 get in for free. On Wednesday nights, from 6 PM to 9 PM, [2] ______________ is free for everyone. That is called Art Wednesday Nights. We have more than 90,000 artworks in our gallery. The works are from Africa, America, Asia, and Europe. Please remember, you cannot take pictures! There is a special [3] ______________ section, too. Right now that section is showing Rebecca Neilstein's artworks. It ends on May 8th, 2019. The art in the special [4] ______________ changes every 6 months. Do you need a tour of the gallery? There are five tours every day, from 11 AM to 4 PM. There is one tour every hour. One tour takes about 40 minutes. The tours are always free! For more [5] ______________ about the Art Gallery of Saint Peter, visit our [6] ______________ at www.saintpeterart.org.

Word Bank

openuntil	intry	secion
open until	inpormation	artwork
section	entry	information
website	atwork	webesit

Listen. Pause. Say each sentence.

MP3 B2-9G

Writing Practice

Write the words.

1 ______________ ex Is the store ______ 9 PM? Then it closes its doors at 9 PM.	2 ______________ n going in
3 ______________ n a piece of art	4 ______________ n area
5 ______________ to learn more about	6 ______________ n page on the internet

Write the words in each blank.

Summary

The Art Gallery of Saint Peter ______________ everyone. On Wednesday nights, ______________ is ______________. We are now showing Rebecca Neilstein's artworks. You can also take a free gallery ______________.

Word Puzzle

Complete the word puzzle.

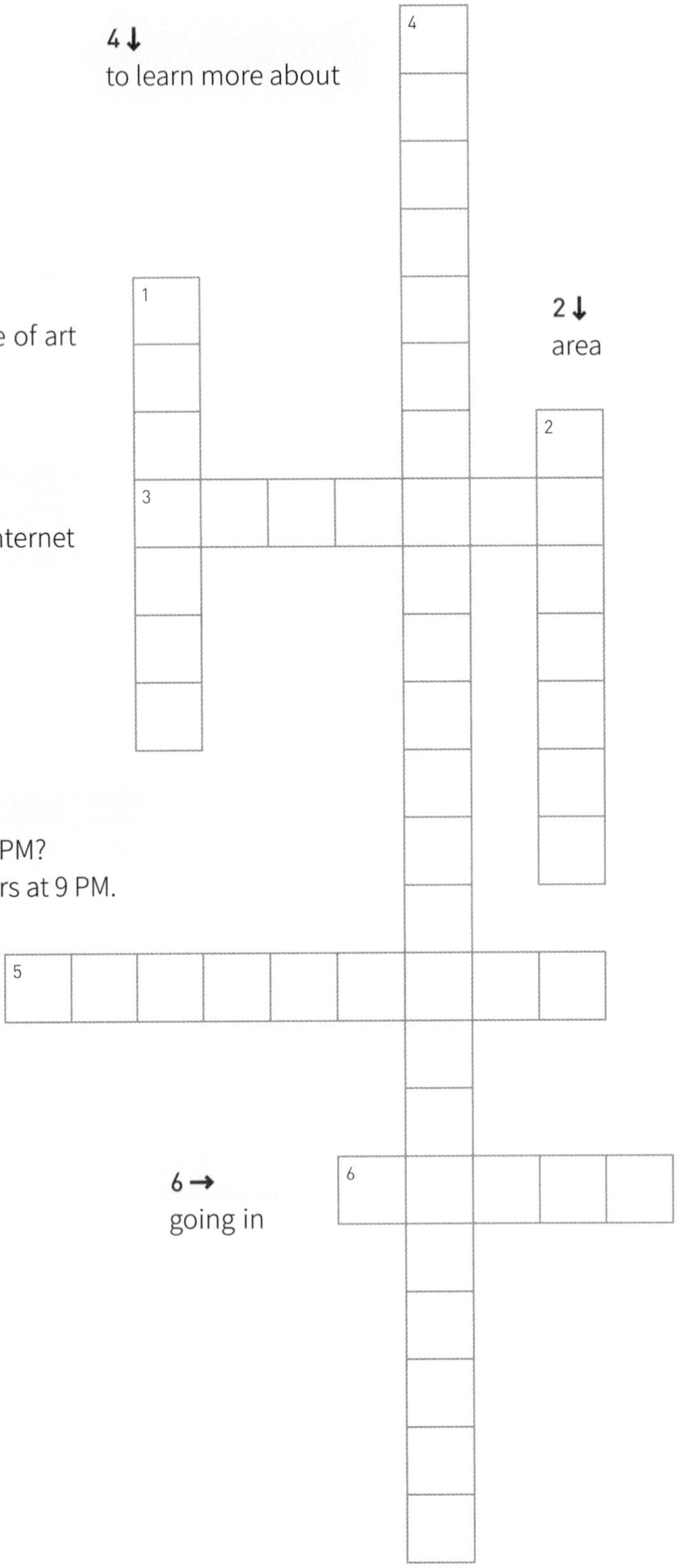

4↓
to learn more about

1↓
a piece of art

2↓
area

3→
page on the internet

5→
Is the store _______ 9 PM?
Then it closes its doors at 9 PM.

6→
going in

Teacher's Book
p.138

UNIT 10

What Is Origami?

Do you like folding paper?
What can you make out of paper?

UNIT 10 What Is Origami?

Origami first started in China, but the word "origami" comes from Japan. It means paper folding. People can make masks, animals, and toys by folding paper. But origami is not just about folding paper. It is art! Many people enjoy origami as a hobby. They like folding the paper very carefully to make pretty shapes. Workers at stores use origami, too. They fold gift boxes and ribbons. Sometimes they put many folded origami shapes on one piece of string. Then they can decorate their store.

There are many types of paper for origami. Many people like to use shiny paper. Then they can make bright shapes, like stars or flowers. Some people like to use rainbow-colored paper. They make colorful birds and fish. There are also different patterns of origami. Some patterns are easy. Some patterns are very difficult. A dragon or a star pattern might be very hard. But a frog could be an easy pattern.

New Words

fold

v Is she cutting paper in half? No, she is folding it.

gift

n a present

colorful

adj bright and with many colors

string

n very thin rope

decorate X

v make X look beautiful

pattern

n a design

10 minutes

Part A. Sentence Completion

1. Cakes are hard ________, but cookies are easy.

   (A) bake
   (B) baking
   (C) to bake
   (D) to baking

2. Look at that big pile of ________ gifts!

   (A) color
   (B) colors
   (C) colorful
   (D) colorfully

Part B. Situational Writing

3.

He is ________ his shirts.

   (A) folding
   (B) sewing
   (C) painting
   (D) washing

4.

The cat is playing with some ________.

   (A) mice
   (B) water
   (C) string
   (D) robots

Part C. Practical Reading and Retelling

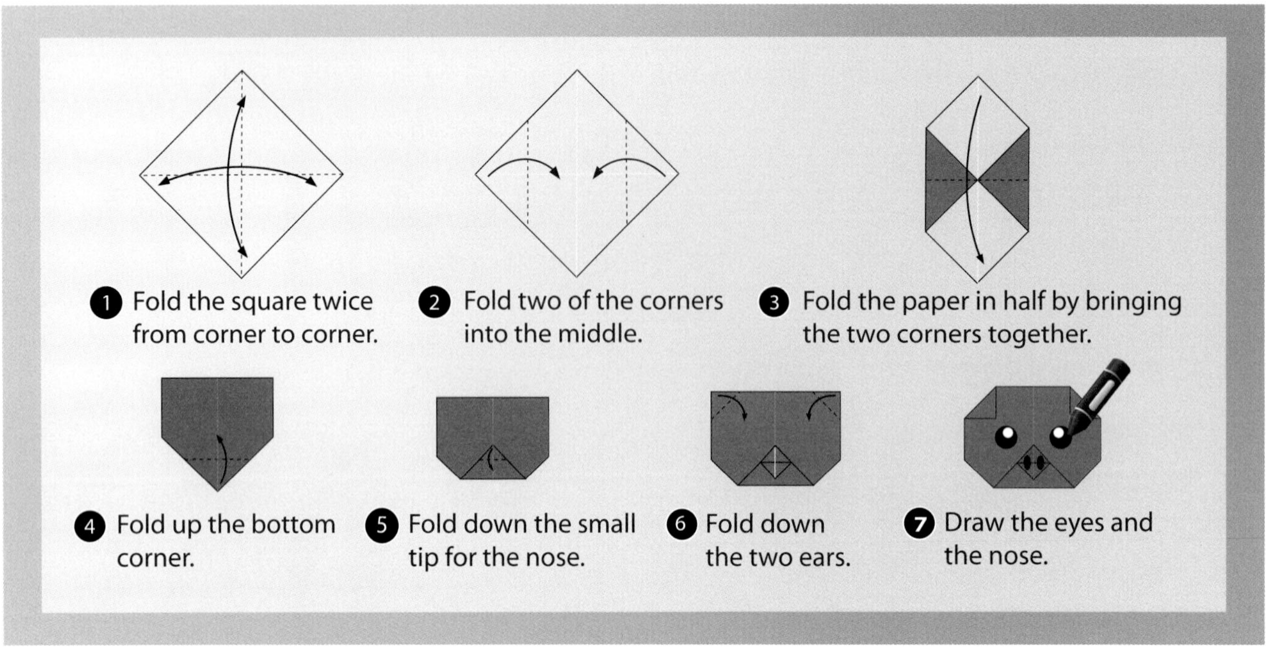

5. When do you fold the ears?

(A) in the last step
(B) after drawing the eyes
(C) after folding down the nose
(D) before folding the paper in half

6. For which step do you need a crayon?

(A) 1
(B) 3
(C) 4
(D) 7

Part D. General Reading and Retelling

Origami first started in China, but the word "origami" comes from Japan. It means paper folding. People can make masks, animals, and toys by folding paper. But origami is not just about folding paper. It is art! Many people enjoy origami as a hobby. They like folding the paper very carefully to make pretty shapes. Workers at stores use origami, too. They fold gift boxes and ribbons. Sometimes they put many folded origami shapes on one piece of string. Then they can decorate their store.

There are many types of paper for origami. Many people like to use shiny paper. Then they can make bright shapes, like stars or flowers. Some people like to use rainbow-colored paper. They make colorful birds and fish. There are also different patterns of origami. Some patterns are easy. Some patterns are very difficult. A dragon or a star pattern might be very hard. But a frog could be an easy pattern.

7. What is the best title for the passage?

(A) Find Your Favorite Hobby
(B) Paper Bags and Plastic Bags
(C) Folding Paper for Many Things
(D) Why Students Don't Like Origami

8. According to the passage, what is NOT true about origami?

(A) It is a type of art.
(B) It started in Japan.
(C) It means folding paper.
(D) It is a hobby for some people.

9. Which origami pattern is mentioned in the passage?

(A) school
(B) planet
(C) dragon
(D) mermaid

10. According to the passage, which pattern might be easy?

(A) star
(B) frog
(C) store
(D) gift box

Listening Practice

Listen and write.

MP3 B2-10

What Is Origami?

Origami first started in China, but the word "origami" comes from Japan. It means paper folding. People can make masks, animals, and toys by folding paper. But origami is not just about folding paper. It is art! Many people enjoy origami as a hobby. They like folding the paper very carefully to make pretty shapes. Workers at stores use origami, too. They [1] ______ [2] ______ boxes and ribbons. Sometimes they put many folded origami shapes on one piece of [3] ______. Then they can [4] ______ their store.

There are many types of paper for origami. Many people like to use shiny paper. Then they can make bright shapes, like stars or flowers. Some people like to use rainbow-colored paper. They make [5] ______ birds and fish. There are also different patterns of origami. Some patterns are easy. Some patterns are very difficult. A dragon or a star [6] ______ might be very hard. But a frog could be an easy pattern.

Word Bank

coloful	strinng	string
gifft	gift	patern
pattern	decorate	colorful
pold	fold	decerate

Listen. Pause. Say each sentence.

MP3 B2-10G

Writing Practice

Write the words.

1 ________ *v* Is she cutting paper in half? No, she is ______ing it.	2 ________ *n* a present
3 ________ *adj* bright and with many colors	4 ________ *n* very thin rope
5 ________ X *v* make X look beautiful	6 ________ *n* a design

Write the words in each blank.

Summary

Origami is paper ________________. People like it as art, as a hobby, and for gift ________________. Some people put them on a ________________ of string. There are many types of paper, shapes, and ________________ in origami.

Word Puzzle

Complete the word puzzle.

3↓
Is she cutting paper in half? No, she is ______ing it.

1↓
a design

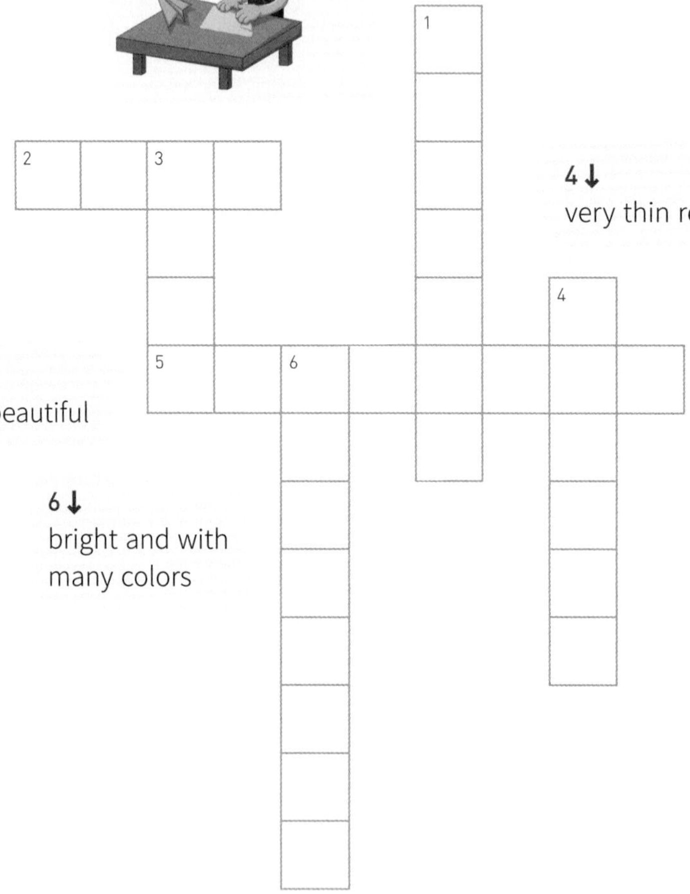

2→
a present

4↓
very thin rope

5→
make X look beautiful

6↓
bright and with many colors

Teacher's Book
p.142

UNIT 11

Introduction to Webtoons

Do you like reading comics? Do you read comics online?

UNIT 11 Introduction to Webtoons

What is a webtoon? The word "webtoon" is from "web" and "cartoon," so a webtoon is an online cartoon, or comic. The first webtoon was made in 2003. A Korean company called Daum made it. From 2004, other companies began to make webtoons, too. Each week, the artists draw a new story. Sometimes the story is free, and sometimes the reader needs to pay money. Many people read webtoons online. About 10 million people read free webtoons in 2016. As people read webtoons, they become fans of the artists. Some artists are really famous for their webtoons. They sometimes appear on TV!

Do you want to become a webtoon artist? Then draw a free webtoon and put it on a webtoon site. Maybe a company will ask you to join it. The company will pay you after you join. Do many readers like your webtoon? Then you will get more money. But drawing a new story every week is not easy. Some artists get neck pain from drawing. Sometimes, artists have to draw for ten hours a day!

New Words

cartoon *n* a comic book	begin *v* start
company *n* a business	become fans of *v* start to like a lot
neck pain *n* a hurt neck	ten hours a day *n* ten hours every day

Part A. Sentence Completion

1. Each ________, I go to karate lessons.

(A) week
(B) weeks
(C) a week
(D) my week

2. My brothers have to ________ at least eight hours a day.

(A) sleep
(B) be sleep
(C) sleeping
(D) is sleeps

Part B. Situational Writing

3.

Nila has ________.

(A) neck pain
(B) a paper cut
(C) a broken leg
(D) stomach pain

4.

Nick is ________ on the screen.

(A) showing a car
(B) drawing a cartoon
(C) spilling some coffee
(D) watching a baseball game

5. How many stories should you draw for the competition?

(A) 2

(B) 3

(C) 6

(D) 8

6. What is NOT true about the contest?

(A) The winner gets $50,000.

(B) The artist must color the work.

(C) A 15-year-old student can join.

(D) There are more than 7 types of webtoon.

Part D. General Reading and Retelling

What is a webtoon? The word “webtoon” is from “web” and “cartoon,” so a webtoon is an online cartoon, or comic. The first webtoon was made in 2003. A Korean company called Daum made it. From 2004, other companies began to make webtoons, too. Each week, the artists draw a new story. Sometimes the story is free, and sometimes the reader needs to pay money. Many people read webtoons online. About 10 million people read free webtoons in 2016. As people read webtoons, they become fans of the artists. Some artists are really famous for their webtoons. They sometimes appear on TV!

Do you want to become a webtoon artist? Then draw a free webtoon and put it on a webtoon site. Maybe a company will ask you to join it. The company will pay you after you join. Do many readers like your webtoon? Then you will get more money. But drawing a new story every week is not easy. Some artists get neck pain from drawing. Sometimes, artists have to draw for ten hours a day!

7. What is this passage mainly about?
   - (A) TV shows from Korea
   - (B) famous cartoon artists
   - (C) webtoons and their artists
   - (D) the most popular websites

8. According to the passage, when did the first webtoon start?
   - (A) in 2003
   - (B) in 2004
   - (C) in 2010
   - (D) in 2016

9. According to the passage, what should you do first to become a webtoon artist?
   - (A) look for a company
   - (B) cure your neck pain
   - (C) draw free webtoons
   - (D) ask companies to pay

10. According to the passage, why do some webtoon artists have neck pain?
    - (A) They walk very fast.
    - (B) They do not sleep well.
    - (C) They watch too much TV.
    - (D) They draw for a long time.

Listening Practice

Listen and write.

MP3 B2-11

Introduction to Webtoons

What is a webtoon? The word "webtoon" is from "web" and "1 ____________," so a webtoon is an online cartoon, or comic. The first webtoon was made in 2003. A Korean 2 ____________ called Daum made it. From 2004, other companies 3 ____________ to make webtoons, too. Each week, the artists draw a new story. Sometimes the story is free, and sometimes the reader needs to pay money. Many people read webtoons online. About 10 million people read free webtoons in 2016. As people read webtoons, they become 4 ____________ the artists. Some artists are really famous for their webtoons. They sometimes appear on TV!

Do you want to become a webtoon artist? Then draw a free webtoon and put it on a webtoon site. Maybe a company will ask you to join it. The company will pay you after you join. Do many readers like your webtoon? Then you will get more money. But drawing a new story every week is not easy. Some artists get 5 ____________ from drawing. Sometimes, artists have to draw for ten hours 6 ____________!

Word Bank

catoon	aday	began
company	begin	fans of
compeny	cartoon	a day
neck pain	pans of	nek pein

Listen. Pause. Say each sentence.

MP3 B2-11G

Writing Practice

Write the words.

1 ________ *n* a comic book	2 ________ *v* start
3 ________ *n* a business	4 ________ *v* start to like a lot
5 ________ *n* a hurt neck	6 ________ *n* ten hours every day

Write the words in each blank.

Summary

A webtoon is an online ________________. Webtoons started in ______________ in 2003. Webtoon ________________ have many fans. The artists can become ________________, but the work can be hard.

Word Puzzle

Complete the word puzzle.

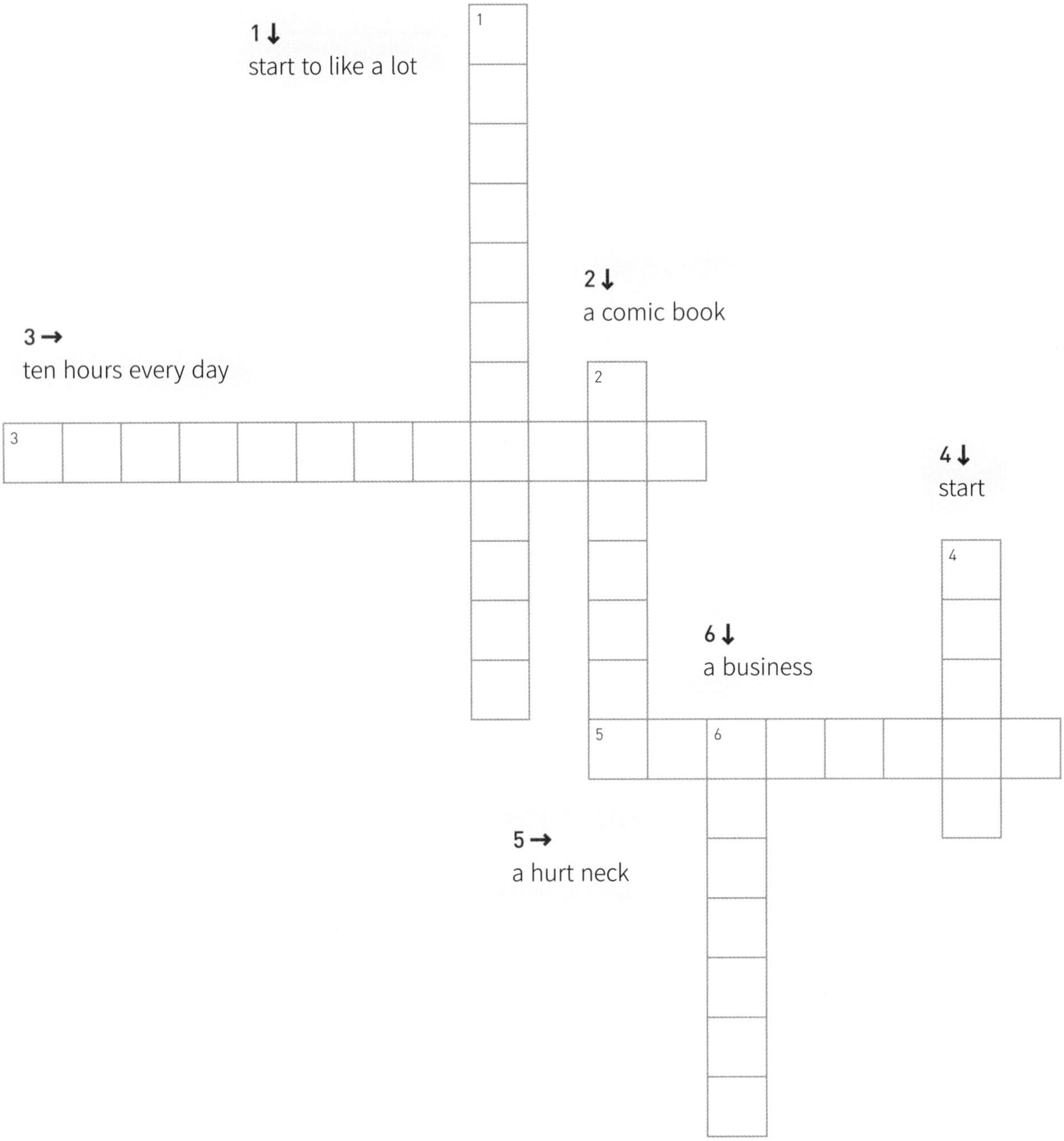

1↓
start to like a lot

2↓
a comic book

3→
ten hours every day

4↓
start

5→
a hurt neck

6↓
a business

Teacher's Book p.147

UNIT 12

Haihat's Recycled Pig

What can you make with an old bottle or can?

UNIT 12 Haihat's Recycled Pig

Haihat bought many things, so she had a lot of trash in her house. She had plastic bottles, paper boxes, clothes, and cans. She wanted to use them. Then, she remembered last week's art class. In class, the teacher, Mr. Thal, showed pictures of recycled art. The artists used trash to make recycled art. Trash became something beautiful! So, Haihat collected three plastic bottles and some clothes. She thought of some animals. She thought, "A bottle lid looks like a pig's nose!" Haihat decided to make plastic pigs. She asked her dad to help her. That's because cutting plastic is dangerous. Haihat's dad cut the plastic bottles. They became the pigs' ears. He also cut the lid for the noses. Then, Haihat cut the clothes. She glued them on the pigs. Finally, she colored the pigs pink and put two big eyes on each one. The trash became a piece of art. Haihat took a picture of her pigs. Then, she showed it to Mr. Thal. Mr. Thal was happy to see the photo. He told Haihat to bring the pigs to class next week.

New Words

recycle *v* use things again	**lid** *n* the top of a bottle
dangerous *adj* not safe	**look like** *v* look the same as
glue *v* use sticky stuff to put together	**piece of art** *n* an artwork

10 minutes

Part A. Sentence Completion

1. A rope sometimes looks _______ a snake.

   (A) is
   (B) like
   (C) that
   (D) may

2. Dad cut a _______ for me.

   (A) light cans
   (B) paper box
   (C) glue sticks
   (D) plastic bottles

Part B. Situational Writing

3. 

   The flowers are _______ the boots.

   (A) right inside
   (B) right behind
   (C) directly under
   (D) just to the left of

4. 

   Yuki likes to _______.

   (A) paint her walls
   (B) cut plastic pieces
   (C) glue pieces of paper
   (D) take pictures outside

Recycled Art

Name: Yuri

My Artwork

Comments from Classmates

I like...

Jaleb: The noses are really cute.
Wyatt: I like the yellow pig with the red nose.

Maybe next time...

Joao: You can put shiny things in each pig.
Zane: Maybe each pig needs a mouth.

5. Who wrote about putting things in a bottle?

(A) Jaleb
(B) Wyatt
(C) Joao
(D) Zane

6. What does Zane think?

(A) The eyes are too big.
(B) The colors are bright.
(C) Each pig needs a mouth.
(D) Each pig needs bigger ears.

Part D. General Reading and Retelling

Haihat bought many things, so she had a lot of trash in her house. She had plastic bottles, paper boxes, clothes, and cans. She wanted to use them. Then, she remembered last week's art class. In class, the teacher, Mr. Thal, showed pictures of recycled art. The artists used trash to make recycled art. Trash became something beautiful! So, Haihat collected three plastic bottles and some clothes. She thought of some animals. She thought, "A bottle lid looks like a pig's nose!" Haihat decided to make plastic pigs. She asked her dad to help her. That's because cutting plastic is dangerous. Haihat's dad cut the plastic bottles. They became the pigs' ears. He also cut the lid for the noses. Then, Haihat cut the clothes. She glued them on the pigs. Finally, she colored the pigs pink and put two big eyes on each one. The trash became a piece of art. Haihat took a picture of her pigs. Then, she showed it to Mr. Thal. Mr. Thal was happy to see the photo. He told Haihat to bring the pigs to class next week.

7. What is the main idea of the passage?

(A) Adults can cut plastic.
(B) Haihat made recycled art.
(C) Plastic bottles have good lids.
(D) Mr. Thal is the best art teacher.

8. Who is Mr. Thal?

(A) Haihat's dad
(B) a store owner
(C) an art teacher
(D) a bottle maker

9. Why did Haihat make pigs?

(A) Cans looked perfect for pigs.
(B) Her dad told her to make pigs.
(C) She had some big glass bottles.
(D) A bottle lid looked like a pig's nose.

10. What did Haihat do with the pigs?

(A) paint them white
(B) put them in the trash
(C) take a photo of them
(D) bring them to art class

Listening Practice

Listen and write.

MP3 B2-12

Haihat's Recycled Pig

Haihat bought many things, so she had a lot of trash in her house. She had plastic bottles, paper boxes, clothes, and cans. She wanted to use them. Then, she remembered last week's art class. In class, the teacher, Mr. Thal, showed pictures of [1] ______ art. The artists used trash to make recycled art. Trash became something beautiful! So, Haihat collected three plastic bottles and some clothes. She thought of some animals. She thought, "A bottle lid [2] ______ a pig's nose!" Haihat decided to make plastic pigs. She asked her dad to help her. That's because cutting plastic is [3] ______. Haihat's dad cut the plastic bottles. They became the pigs' ears. He also cut the [4] ______ for the noses. Then, Haihat cut the clothes. She [5] ______ them on the pigs. Finally, she colored the pigs pink and put two big eyes on each one. The trash became a [6] ______. Haihat took a picture of her pigs. Then, she showed it to Mr. Thal. Mr. Thal was happy to see the photo. He told Haihat to bring the pigs to class next week.

Word Bank

glood	looks like	piece of art
lid	recycled	resicled
dangrous	lookslike	rid
dangerous	glued	peace of art

Listen. Pause. Say each sentence.

MP3 B2-12G

Writing Practice

Write the words.

1 ______________ *v* use things again	2 ______________ *n* the top of a bottle
3 ______________ *adj* not safe	4 ______________ *v* look the same as
5 ______________ *v* use sticky stuff to put together	6 ______________ *n* an artwork

Write the words in each blank.

Summary

Haihat wanted to use her ______________. She remembered beautiful ______________ art from her class. So she collected some trash to make plastic ______________. Her ______________ teacher liked the pigs.

Word Puzzle

Complete the word puzzle.

1 → the top of a bottle

2 ↓ not safe

3 ↓ an artwork

4 → use things again

5 ↓ look the same as

6 → use sticky stuff to put together

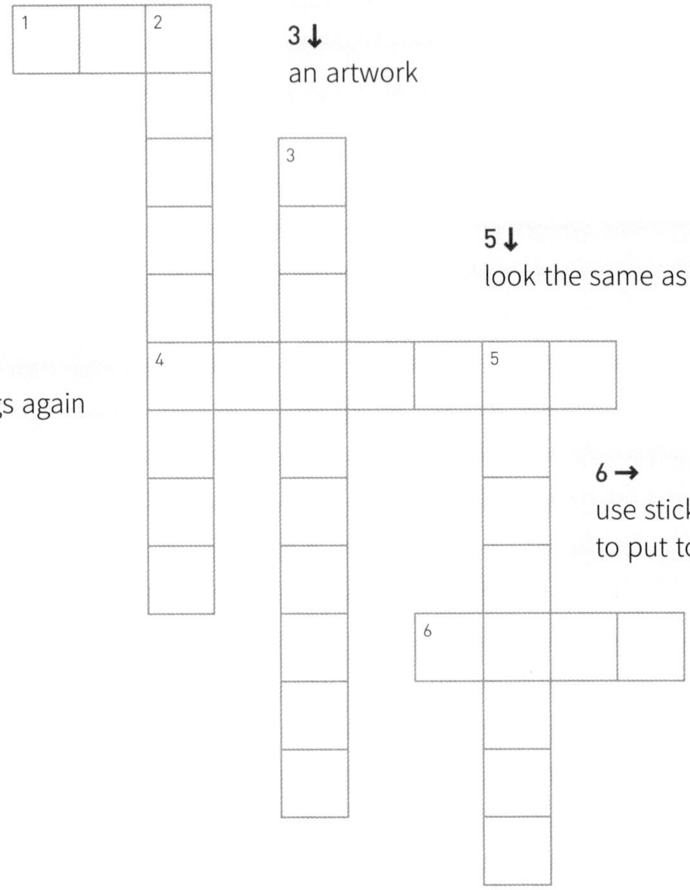

CHAPTER REVIEW

The Court Artist's Rooster

Teacher's Book p.151

Once upon a time, there was a king. He loved roosters[1] and thought they were beautiful. So one day, he said to the court artist, "Paint a picture of a rooster for me." The king waited and waited. In fact, he waited a whole year. Still, there was no picture. The king was angry. "BRING ME THE ARTIST!" he shouted. The artist came out. She had paper, paint, and a paintbrush. She painted a picture of a rooster. It took just five minutes. The king was angrier. His face became purple. He shouted, "Why is this so late? You had one year! And you only do the painting NOW???" The artist was calm. She said, "My king, please come with me." The king followed the artist into a room. The room had 1000 pieces of paper in it. The paper showed pictures of roosters. "See?" said the artist to the king. "I painted a picture in five minutes. But I needed one year to learn how."

[1] rooster

ANSWERS

CHAPTER 1 | Healthy Life
p.10

UNIT 1 B2-1 p.11

1 (A) 2 (C) 3 (B) 4 (D) 5 (D) 6 (D) 7 (D) 8 (C) 9 (A) 10 (C)
1 tips 2 listener 3 in person 4 in real life 5 fight 6 keep
1 tip 2 good listener 3 in person 4 in real life 5 have a fight 6 keep
long, listener, in person, I'm sorry
→ 2 keep 5 in person 6 tip ↓ 1 have a fight 3 in real life 4 good listener

UNIT 2 B2-2 p.19

1 (C) 2 (B) 3 (A) 4 (C) 5 (D) 6 (A) 7 (B) 8 (D) 9 (A) 10 (C)
1 energy 2 barked 3 noticed 4 pet 5 lonely 6 wonderful
1 notice 2 lonely 3 have a lot of energy 4 bark 5 pet 6 wonderful
dog, not, take care of, park
→ 3 notice 5 bark 6 lonely ↓ 1 wonderful 2 pet 4 have a lot of energy

UNIT 3 B2-3 p.27

1 (C) 2 (A) 3 (B) 4 (C) 5 (C) 6 (B) 7 (A) 8 (C) 9 (B) 10 (D)
1 tissues 2 allergy 3 water 4 pollen 5 runny nose 6 go away
1 tissue 2 allergy 3 your eyes water 4 pollen 5 runny nose 6 go away
grass, summer, tissues, windows
→ 5 runny nose 6 allergy ↓ 1 pollen 2 go away 3 your eyes water 4 tissue

UNIT 4 B2-4 p.35

1 (A) 2 (A) 3 (A) 4 (D) 5 (D) 6 (B) 7 (D) 8 (C) 9 (B) 10 (C)
1 look down at 2 in trouble 3 spine 4 advice 5 experts 6 stretch
1 look down at 2 in trouble 3 spine 4 advice 5 expert 6 stretch
down, spine, up, stretch
→ 1 in trouble 3 advice 6 expert ↓ 2 look down at 4 stretch 5 spine

CHAPTER 2 | Food Trend
p.44

UNIT 5 B2-5 p.45

1 (D) 2 (B) 3 (A) 4 (D) 5 (D) 6 (C) 7 (C) 8 (D) 9 (D) 10 (C)
1 invention 2 Hawaiian 3 inventor 4 tasted 5 slices 6 can
1 invention 2 Hawaiian 3 inventor 4 taste 5 can 6 slice
inventor, pineapple, sweet, like
→ 2 slice 3 inventor 4 can 5 Hawaiian ↓ 1 taste 3 invention

UNIT 6 B2-6 p.53

1 (B) 2 (B) 3 (A) 4 (C) 5 (D) 6 (C) 7 (B) 8 (C) 9 (C) 10 (D)
1 meals 2 snack 3 healthy 4 calories 5 fast food 6 tacos
1 meal 2 calorie 3 snack 4 taco 5 fast food 6 healthy
meal, not, food, healthy
→ 4 snack 5 meal 6 taco ↓ 1 fast food 2 healthy 3 calorie

UNIT 7 B2-7 p.61

1 (B) 2 (C) 3 (D) 4 (B) 5 (B) 6 (D) 7 (D) 8 (C) 9 (B) 10 (C)
1 local 2 fresh 3 truck 4 dirt 5 seeds 6 At that point
1 local 2 fresh 3 dirt 4 truck 5 at that point 6 seed
local, said, grow, tomatoes
→ 1 fresh 4 dirt 5 truck 6 local ↓ 2 seed 3 at that point

UNIT 8 B2-8 p.69

1 (C) 2 (C) 3 (D) 4 (C) 5 (A) 6 (D) 7 (C) 8 (C) 9 (D) 10 (A)
1 avocado 2 ripe 3 hard 4 overripe 5 in half 6 scoop
1 avocado 2 ripe 3 hard 4 overripe 5 in half 6 scoop out
color, half, seed, Scoop
→ 2 scoop out 4 hard 5 cut in half 6 ripe ↓ 1 avocado 3 overripe

CHAPTER 3 | Arts and Crafts
p.78

UNIT 9 B2-9 p.79

1 (A) 2 (C) 3 (D) 4 (B) 5 (A) 6 (B) 7 (D) 8 (A) 9 (A) 10 (C)
1 open until 2 entry 3 artwork 4 section 5 information 6 website
1 open until 2 entry 3 artwork 4 section 5 for more information about 6 website
welcomes, entry, free, tour
→ 3 website 5 open until 6 entry ↓ 1 artwork 2 section 4 for more information about

UNIT 10 B2-10 p.87

1 (C) 2 (C) 3 (A) 4 (C) 5 (C) 6 (D) 7 (C) 8 (B) 9 (C) 10 (B)
1 fold 2 gift 3 string 4 decorate 5 colorful 6 pattern
1 fold 2 gift 3 colorful 4 string 5 decorate 6 pattern
folding, boxes, piece, patterns
→ 2 gift 5 decorate ↓ 1 pattern 3 fold 4 string 6 colorful

UNIT 11 B2-11 p.95

1 (A) 2 (A) 3 (A) 4 (B) 5 (C) 6 (D) 7 (C) 8 (A) 9 (C) 10 (D)
1 cartoon 2 company 3 began 4 fans of 5 neck pain 6 a day
1 cartoon 2 begin 3 company 4 become fans of 5 neck pain 6 ten hours a day
cartoon, Korea, artists, famous
→ 3 ten hours a day 5 neck pain ↓ 1 become fans of 2 cartoon 4 begin 6 company

UNIT 12 B2-12 p.103

1 (B) 2 (B) 3 (A) 4 (C) 5 (C) 6 (C) 7 (B) 8 (C) 9 (D) 10 (C)
1 recycled 2 looks like 3 dangerous 4 lid 5 glued 6 piece of art
1 recycle 2 lid 3 dangerous 4 look like 5 glue 6 piece of art
trash, recycled, pigs, art
→ 1 lid 4 recycle 6 glue ↓ 2 dangerous 3 piece of art 5 look like